CONFLICTS OF THE FORTH

Murray Cook & Jim Roche

Other Books by Murray Cook

Rituals, Roundhouses and Romans
[with Lindsay Dunbar]

Digging into Stirling's Past:
Uncovering the Secrets of Scotland's Smallest City

The Anvil of Scottish History: Stories of Stirling

Balbithan Wood, Kintore, Aberdeenshire:
The Evaluation of Prehistoric Landscapes

White Castle:
The Evaluation of an Upstanding Prehistoric Enclosure in East Lothian
[with David Connolly and Hana Kdolska]

Bannockburn and Stirling Bridge:
Exploring Scotland's Two Greatest Battles

The Bannock Burn:
Journeys Along and Across the World's Most Famous Burn
[with Ian McNeish]

Scotland's Christmas:
Festive Celebrations, Traditions and Customs in Scotland
from Samhain to Still Game
[with Thomas A. Christie]

CONFLICTS OF THE FORTH

Exploring 6,000 Years of Warfare at Scotland's Bloodiest Spot

Murray Cook & Jim Roche

Conflicts of the Forth: Exploring 6,000 Years of Warfare at Scotland's Bloodiest Spot by Murray Cook and Jim Roche

First edition published in Great Britain in 2024 by Extremis Publishing Ltd., Suite 218, Castle House, 1 Baker Street, Stirling, FK8 1AL, United Kingdom.

www.extremispublishing.com

Extremis Publishing is a Private Limited Company registered in Scotland (SC509983) whose Registered Office is Suite 218, Castle House, 1 Baker Street, Stirling, FK8 1AL, United Kingdom.

Copyright © Murray Cook and Jim Roche, 2024.

Murray Cook and Jim Roche have asserted the moral right under the Copyright, Designs and Patents Act 1988 to be identified as the authors of this work.

The views expressed in this work are solely those of the authors, and do not necessarily reflect those of the publisher. The publisher hereby disclaims any responsibility for them.

This book is a work of non-fiction. Unless otherwise noted, the authors and the publisher make no explicit guarantees as to the accuracy of the information included in this book and, in some cases, the names of people, places and organisations may have been altered to protect their privacy. All hyperlinks were believed to be live and correctly detailed at the time of publication.

This book may include references to organisations, feature films, television programmes, popular songs, musical bands, novels, reference books, and other creative works, the titles of which are trademarks and/or registered trademarks, and which are the intellectual properties of their respective copyright holders.

All rights reserved. No part of this publication may be reproduced, stored in a retrieval system, or transmitted, in any form or by any means, electronic, mechanical, photocopying, recording or otherwise, without the prior permission in writing of the publisher.

This book is sold subject to the condition that it shall not, by way of trade or otherwise, be lent, re-sold or hired out, or otherwise circulated without the publisher's prior consent in any form of binding or cover other than that in which it is published and without a similar condition including this condition being imposed on the subsequent purchaser.

A CIP catalogue record for this book is available from the British Library.

ISBN: 978-1-7394845-5-2

Typeset in Sorts Mill Goudy, designed by The League of Moveable Type.

Printed and bound in Great Britain by IngramSpark, Chapter House, Pitfield, Kiln Farm, Milton Keynes, MK11 3LW, United Kingdom.

Cover artwork is Copyright © Jim Roche, all rights reserved.

Cover design and book design is Copyright © Thomas A. Christie.

Author images are Copyright © Murray Cook and Jim Roche, all rights reserved.

Internal photographic images are Copyright © Murray Cook and Jim Roche, and are sourced from the authors' private collections unless otherwise stated in the Image Credits section, which forms an extension to this legal page.

The copyrights of third parties are reserved. All third party imagery is used under the provision of Fair Use for the purposes of commentary and criticism. While every reasonable effort has been made to contact copyright holders and secure permission for all images reproduced in this work, we offer apologies for any instances in which this was not possible and for any inadvertent omissions.

Introduction	Page i
Map of Stirling Town Centre	Page iv
Map of Bannockburn Area	Page vi
Map of Stirling and Environs	Page viii
Conflicts of the Forth	Page 1
Conclusion	Page 109
Endnotes	Page 110
Image Credits	Page 113
About the Authors	Page 119

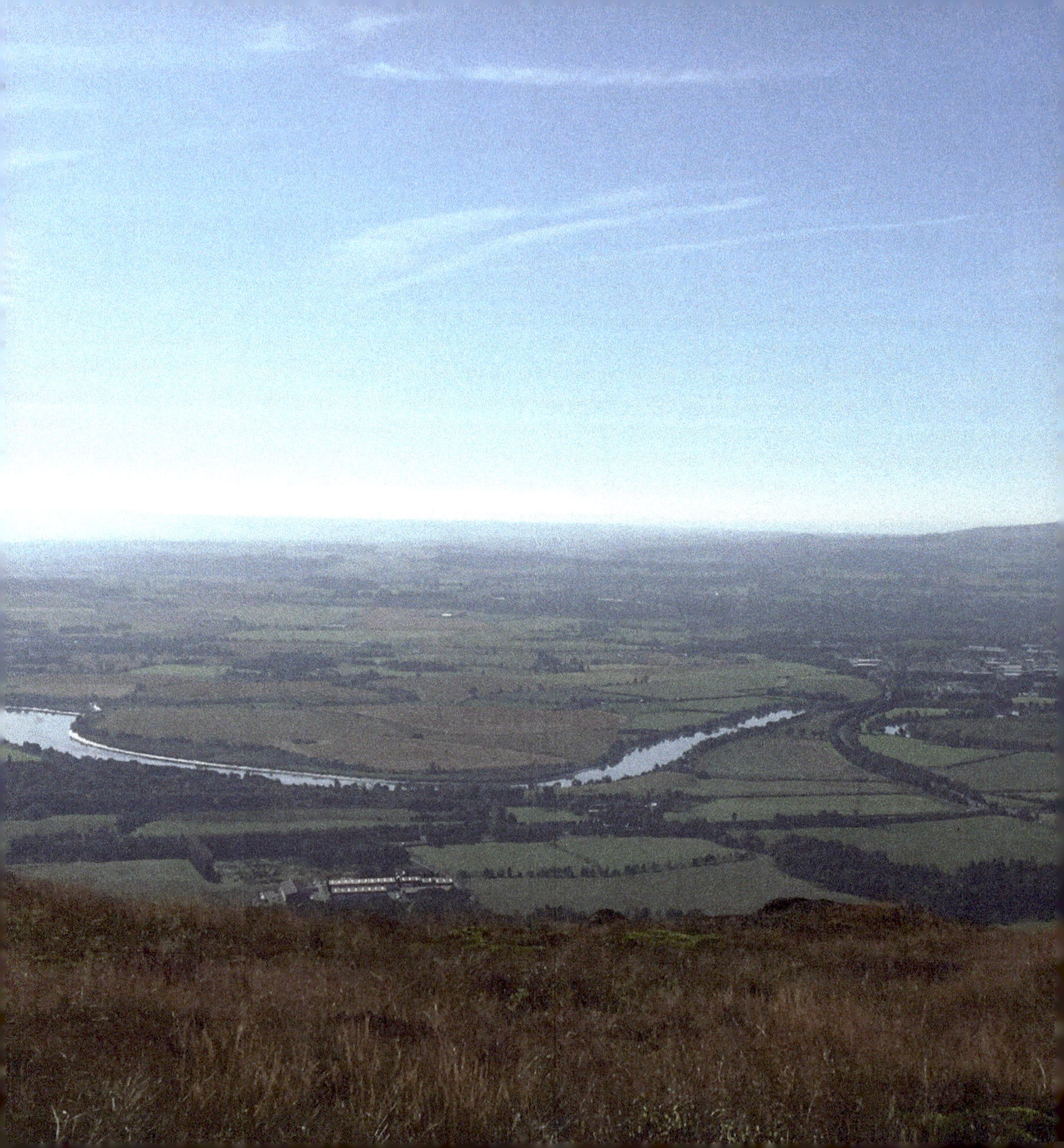

Introduction

A hard military fact throughout Scotland's long and bloody history is that if you wanted to move an army north or south on foot, you had to cross the River Forth at or near Stirling—and thus if you wanted to stop such an invasion, you did it at Stirling. This logic applied to every recorded invasion from the Romans to the Jacobites and including Picts, Angles, Vikings, Edwards I and II, Cromwell and the Duke of Cumberland. At no other place in Scottish history has so much blood been spilled to control such a tiny location. After the Union with England, Stirling Castle became a barracks, and the soldiers and regiments played key roles across the British Empire and its campaigns.

This small book is aimed at the general reader and explores these conflicts, the people who fought in them, and what remains on the ground. We cover the deeper prehistoric past as well as historical events when the area suffered from tribal wars, slavery, invasions, Empire, foreign occupation and civil war, as well as those that fought for Britain across the world, the two World Wars and the Cold War. The book's geography focuses on Stirling and an area 15 miles from it, although once or twice we go to 25 or 30 miles. In the vast majority of our tales there is an actual place to visit, and we give you a ten figure grid reference (if you're used to a six figure one, drop the last two digits off—so NS 79593 98198 would become NS 795 981) and directions if it's at all tricky, but sometimes the location is secret or from a find now in a museum. The stories are presented in chronological order but numbered in explanatory keys to allow you to visit them in clusters. To this end, we have also prepared some maps to help guide you to the locations, all of which were generously compiled by Patrick Roche.

The authors are friends and this book stems from their conversations. Murray is Stirling Council's Archaeologist and often found down a hole researching Stirling's fascinating past. Jim is retired from business and likes 'walking the ground' of battlefields and boring people about the frontage of military units.

The book is designed as an introductory guide to Stirling's military heritage but is absolutely not a comprehensive history of it. It can be taken into the field as you walk or left on the side of the couch, but we hope you explore Stirling's wonderful countryside and enjoy your Right to Roam. This of course means that you can wander anywhere in Scotland except private gardens. But please respect the countryside, don't walk through crops, leave gates as you find them, take your litter home, and keep your dog on the leash.

CONFLICTS OF THE FORTH

Murray Cook
&
Jim Roche

This book is dedicated to the memory of everyone who suffered over the millennia of conflict round Stirling.

We hope and pray for continued peace.

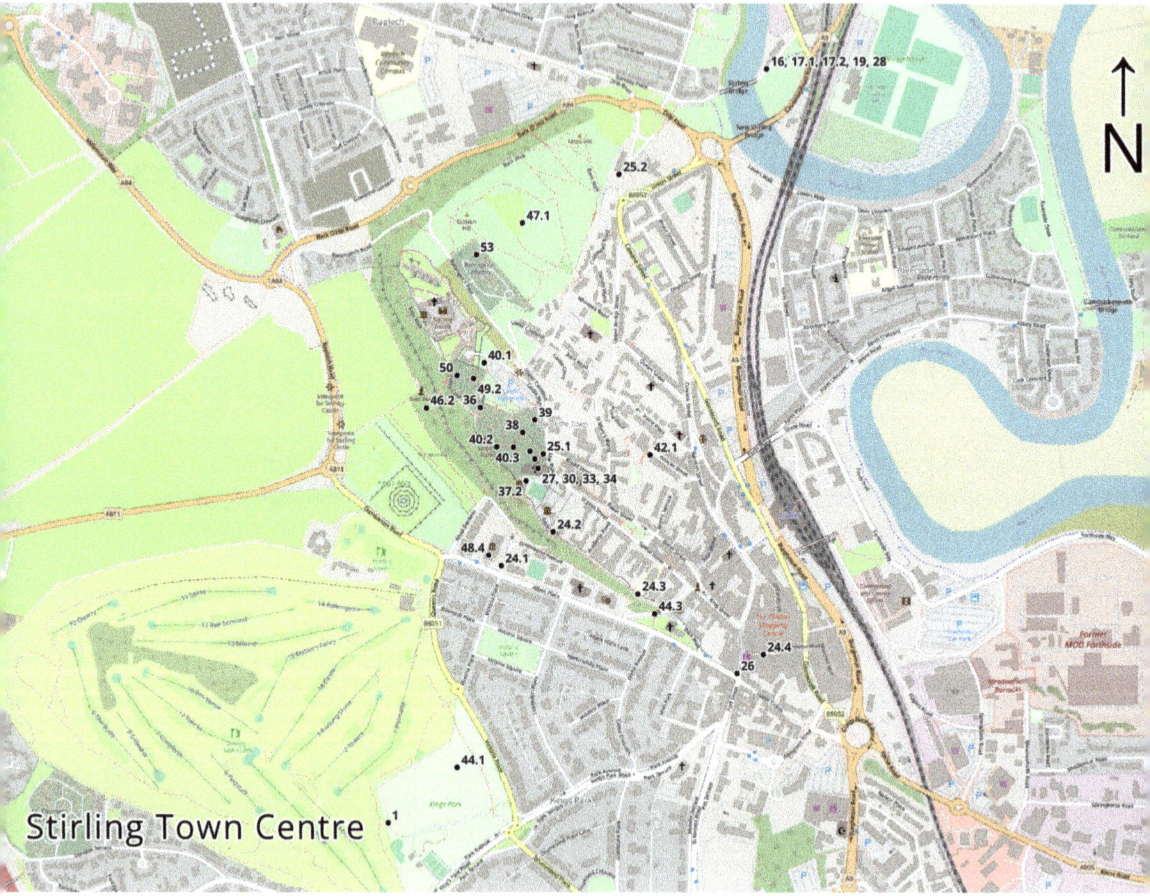
N
16, 17.1, 17.2, 19, 28
25.2
47.1
53
40.1
50
49.2
46.2
36
39
38
40.2
25.1
40.3
27, 30, 33, 34
37.2
42.1
24.2
48.4
24.1
24.3
44.3
24.4
26
44.1
1
Stirling Town Centre

Stirling Town Centre Map

KEY:

- 16 Stirling Bridge: Part 1 (page 32)
- 17 Stirling Bridge: Part 2 (page 33)
- 19 The 1304 Siege of Stirling Castle: Part 1 (page 37)
- 24 Guarding the Rock (page 48)
- 25 Mars Wark (page 49)
- 26 The Battle of Kilsyth (page 52)
- 27 The Church of the Holy Rude (page 53)
- 28 Stirling Bridge: Part 4 (page 56)
- 30 The Battle of Sheriffmuir (page 60)
- 33 Samuel Graham (page 65)
- 34 Marcus Marr (page 68)
- 36 William McGibbon (page 72)
- 37 Private Murphy (page 73)
- 38 'The Indian Mutiny': Part 1 (page 76)
- 39 'The Indian Mutiny': Part 2 (page 77)
- 40 The Boer War (page 80)
- 42 The Territorial Force (page 84)
- 44 The Great War: Part 1 (page 88)
- 46 The Second World War: Part 1 (page 92)
- 47 The Second World War: Part 2 (page 93)
- 48 The Second World War: Part 3 (page 96)
- 49 The Second World War: Part 4 (page 97)
- 50 The Second World War: Part 5 (page 100)
- 53 The Second World War: Part 8 (page 105)

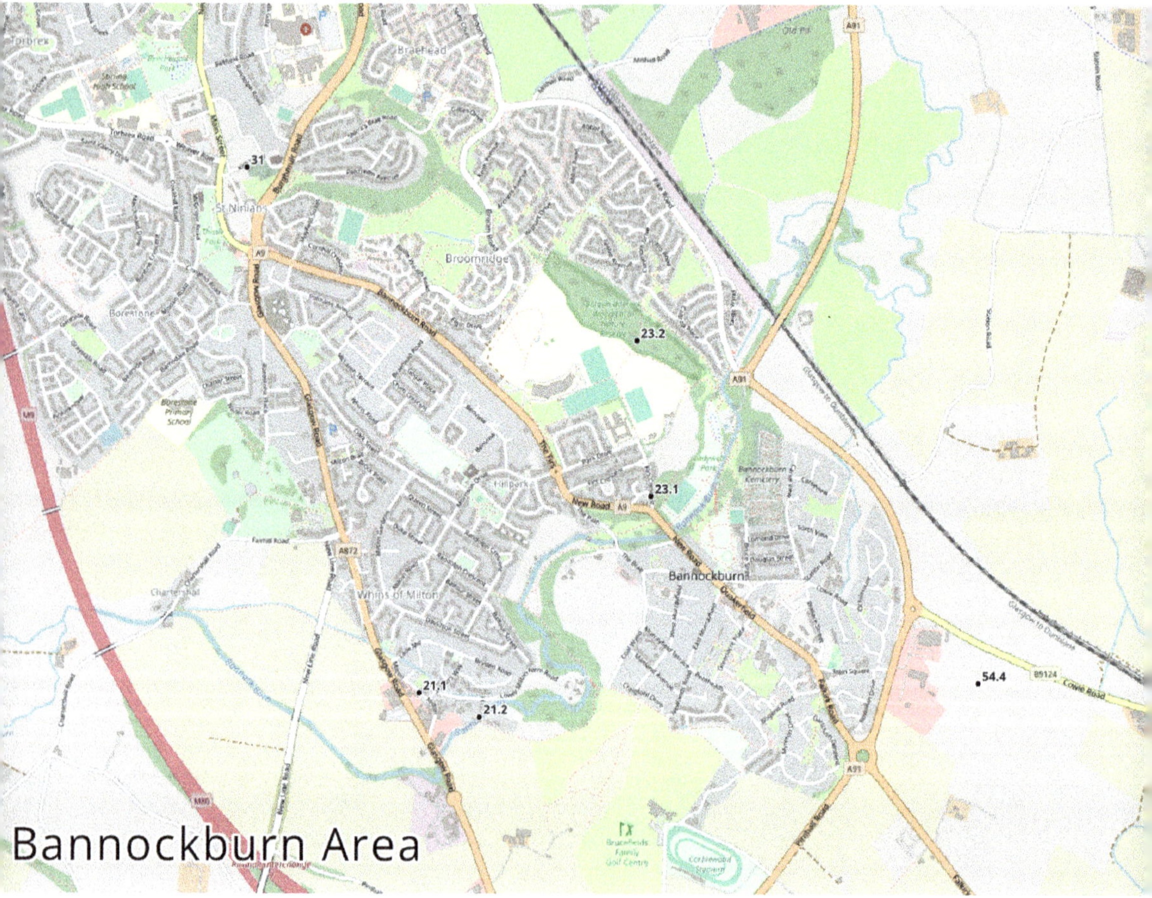
Bannockburn Area
Torbrex
Braehead
St Ninians
Broomridge
Borestone
Whins of Milton
Bannockburn
Hillpark
Chartershall
31
23.2
23.1
21.1
21.2
54.4
A9
A91
A872
B9124
Cowie Road
New Road
Bannockburn Road
Borestone Primary School
Stirling High School
Bannockburn Cemetery
Brucefields Family Golf Centre
Old Pit

Bannockburn Map

KEY:

- **21** Milton Ford (page 41)
- **23** Balquidderock Wood (page 45)
- **31** The '45 (page 61)
- **54** Stirling and the Cold War (page 108)

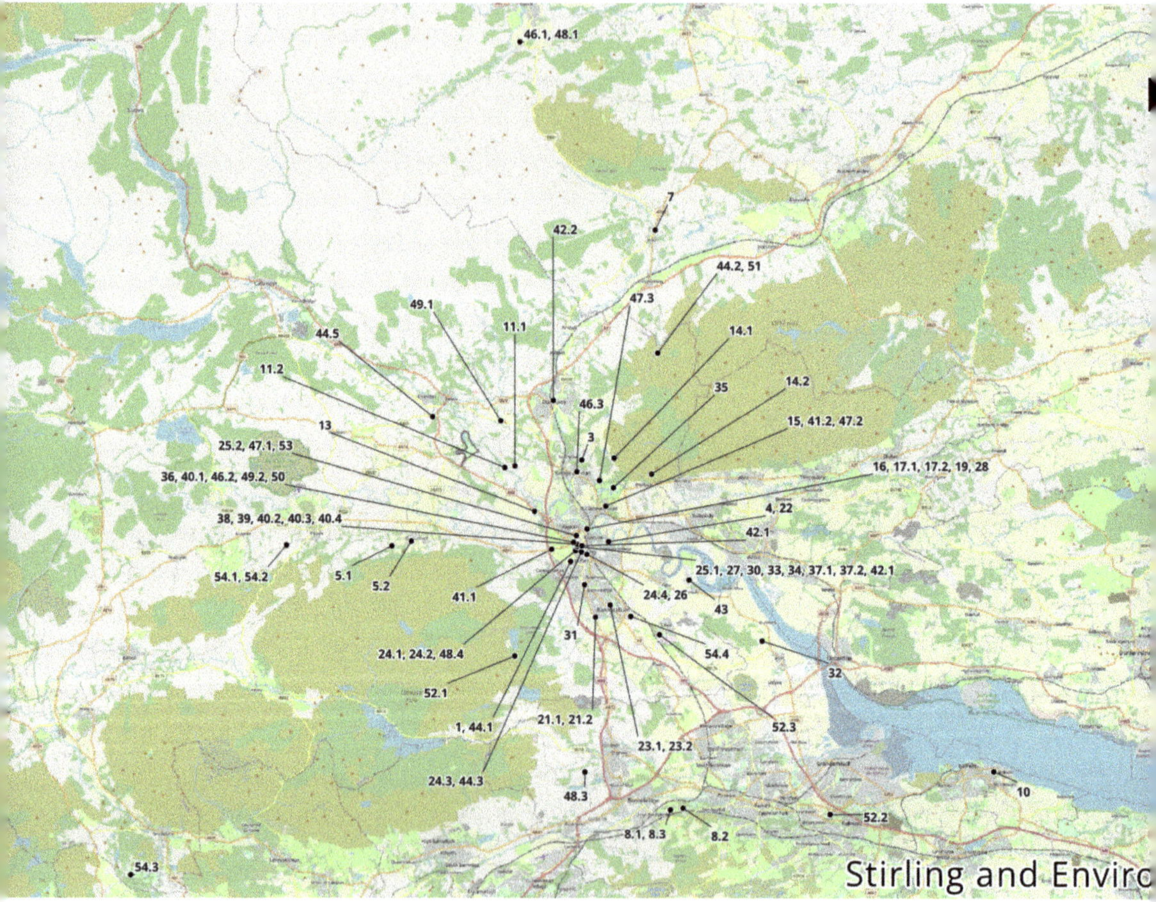
46.1, 48.1
7
42.2
44.2, 51
47.3
49.1
11.1
44.5
14.1
11.2
35
14.2
46.3
15, 41.2, 47.2
13
3
25.2, 47.1, 53
16, 17.1, 17.2, 19, 28
36, 40.1, 46.2, 49.2, 50
4, 22
38, 39, 40.2, 40.3, 40.4
42.1
25.1, 27, 30, 33, 34, 37.1, 37.2, 42.1
54.1, 54.2
5.1
5.2
41.1
24.4, 26
43
31
24.1, 24.2, 48.4
54.4
32
52.1
21.1, 21.2
52.3
1, 44.1
23.1, 23.2
24.3, 44.3
48.3
10
52.2
8.1, 8.3
8.2
54.3
Stirling and Enviro

Map of Stirling and Environs

KEY:

- 1 A Neolithic Hunter (page 1)
- 3 Stirling's First Invader? (page 5)
- 4 The Abbey Ford: Part 1 (page 8)
- 5 Leckie Broch (page 9)
- 7 Ardoch (page 13)
- 8 The Antonine Wall: Part 1 (page 16)
- 10 The Antonine Wall: Part 3 (page 20)
- 11 Ochtertyre Ford: Part 1 (page 21)
- 13 Drip Ford (page 25)
- 14 Dumyat (page 28)
- 15 The Abbey Craig (page 29)
- 16 Stirling Bridge: Part 1 (page 32)
- 17 Stirling Bridge: Part 2 (page 33)
- 19 The 1304 Siege of Stirling Castle: Part 1 (page 37)
- 21 Milton Ford (page 41)
- 22 The Abbey Ford: Part 2 (page 44)
- 23 Balquidderock Wood (page 45)
- 24 Guarding the Rock (page 48)
- 25 Mars Wark (page 49)
- 26 The Battle of Kilsyth (page 52)
- 27 The Church of the Holy Rude (page 53)
- 28 Stirling Bridge: Part 4 (page 56)
- 30 The Battle of Sheriffmuir (page 60)
- 31 The '45 (page 61)
- 32 The 4th Earl of Dunsmore (page 64)
- 33 Samuel Graham (page 65)
- 34 Marcus Marr (page 68)
- 35 Airthrey (page 69)
- 36 William McGibbon (page 72)
- 37 Private Murphy (page 73)
- 38 'The Indian Mutiny': Part 1 (page 76)
- 39 'The Indian Mutiny': Part 2 (page 77)
- 40 The Boer War (page 80)
- 41 The Fighting Cocks (page 81)
- 42 The Territorial Force (page 84)
- 43 Bandeath (page 85)
- 44 The Great War: Part 1 (page 88)
- 46 The Second World War: Part 1 (page 92)
- 47 The Second World War: Part 2 (page 93)
- 48 The Second World War: Part 3 (page 96)
- 49 The Second World War: Part 4 (page 97)
- 50 The Second World War: Part 5 (page 100)
- 51 The Second World War: Part 6 (page 101)
- 52 The Second World War: Part 7 (page 104)
- 53 The Second World War: Part 8 (page 105)
- 54 Stirling and the Cold War (page 108)

A Neolithic Hunter

Our oldest story concerns a 6,000 year old flint arrowhead which was fired at an unknown target in what would become Stirling's Kings Park (NS 78839 92918), the oldest and best-preserved Royal Park in Scotland, founded in the 12th century. The park is now full of dog walkers, families at play and golfers, but its long history contains World War I practice trenches, a 19th century firing range and a Celtic Iron Age fort, built when Stirling was part of the Roman Empire.

Prior to all that, it was simply a hill above a vast inland loch, as 6000 years ago the Forth was higher with dolphins and whales swimming over what is now farmland. This leaf-shaped arrowhead was found by Murray as he monitored a new track being constructed through the park. The sparkling white of the flint contrasted with the dull brown of the mud. It had clearly been fired at something or someone and missed, lost in brush and undergrowth. What we do not know is what or who it was fired at: a deer for the pot or a rival from a different tribe, intent on poaching? Perhaps the aggressor was the poacher. The arrow dates from the Neolithic (from before Bronze and Iron), when in theory our ancestors had taken up farming and abandoned hunting and gathering, so perhaps the arrow reflects a conflict between newly-established farmers and older populations defending their seasonal hunting grounds? Certainly across Neolithic Europe, bows and arrows were used in conflict between people, but we will never know precisely who fired the arrow at what.

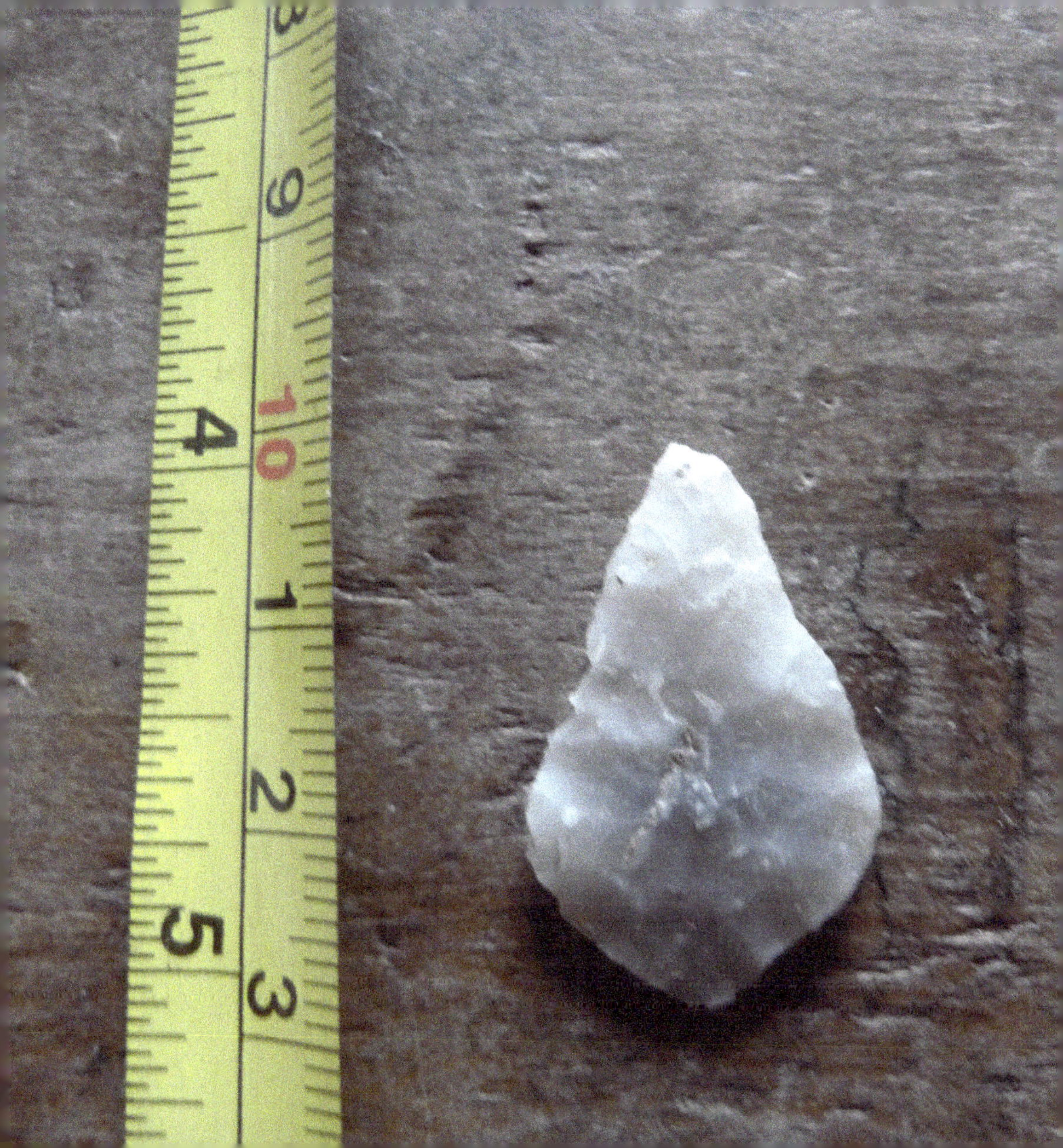

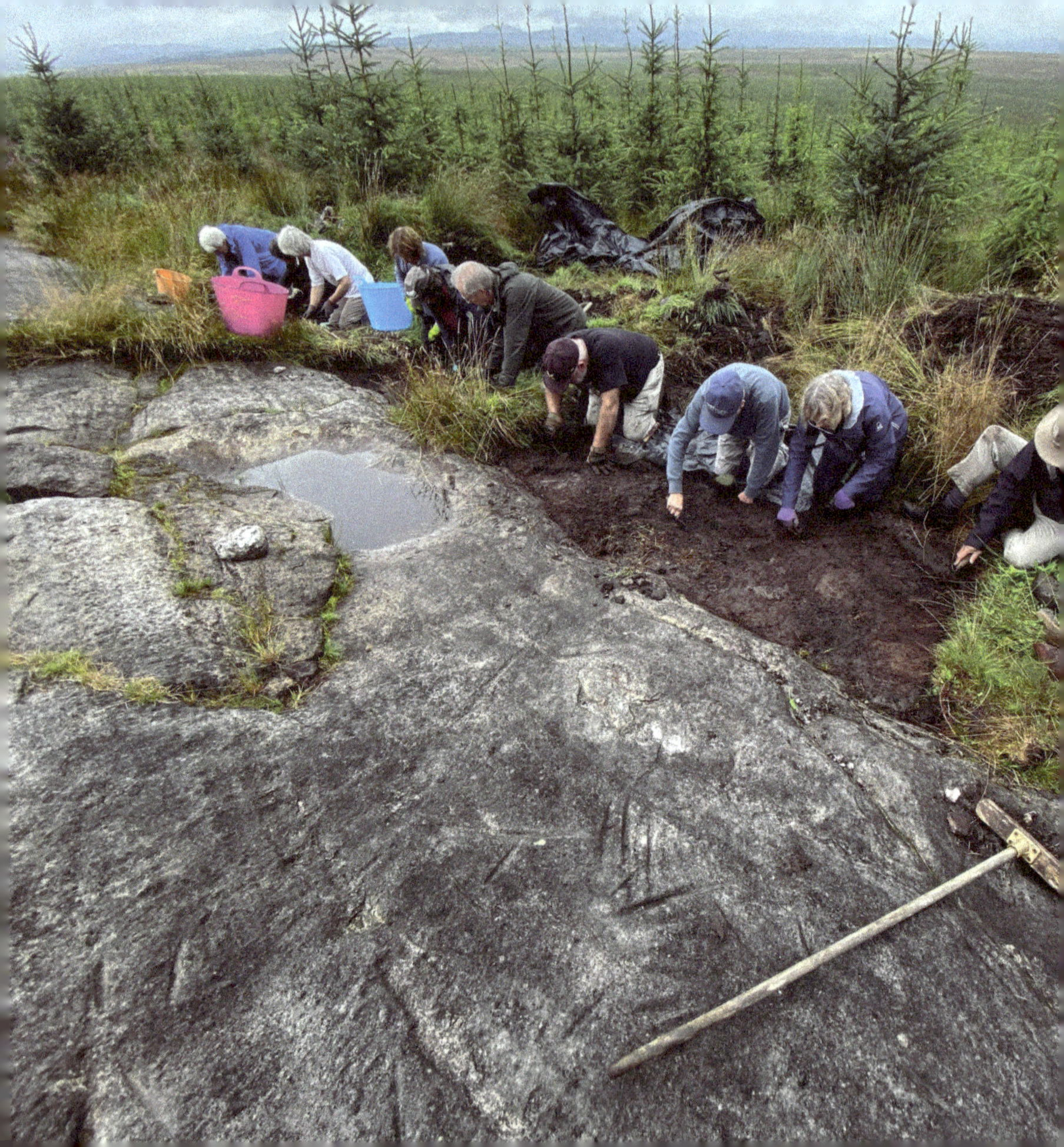

The War on Trees
Britain's Largest Collection of Polissoirs, Found Near Balfron

Now, we are sure you are wondering what a polissoir is? The answer is astonishing: these are grooves made in the living bedrock some 6,000 years ago, used to grind polished stone axes. These were discovered by local man Nick Parish in 2019, and Murray helped record them. They were used to make or sharpen stone axes and, like our arrowhead from King's Park, date to the Neolithic. These axes were not used on people but rather on trees, and over thousands of years helped transform an island covered in woodland to one covered in farms. Despite what you might think, the axes were very efficient and reconstructions suggest it takes 15–30 minutes to chop down a tree.

Now this was not simply the act of an army of prehistoric lumberjacks, but rather a religious and fundamental transformation of the landscape. To our ancestors this appears to have involved the replacement of one set of Gods with another. The axes were often ceremonial items, highly valued and given as gifts; specific stone had to be used, and the finished axes end up all over the country. To date, only two or three polissoirs have been found in Scotland. This might in part be because they have all been destroyed, but it is also because making or sharpening specific axes may have had to be done at specific, special locations. Perhaps you had to undertake a pilgrimage to do it, or to fast, or to do it at a significant and precise time of year. Our grooves show purpose and patterns, parallel and perpendicular lines; maybe family groups or specific axes using the same location for generations? Perhaps each tree felled required an act of atonement?

Stirling's First Invader?
The Fairy Knowe Burial Cairn

For much of the late 19th and 20th century, change and advancement was thought to be achieved through invasion: a stronger, more advanced people conquered the weaker, more primitive races. This was the winning logic of the British Empire, and it was applied to the archaeological record. Britain's first invaders were the Beaker Folk from Europe, and they swept across Britain around 2500–2000 BC with a unique style of pottery (Beakers) and better bronze weaponry. All of Britain's key archaeologists subscribed to this theory, and the main 1940s popular account of our prehistory written by Jacquetta and Christopher describes *'waves of energetic conquerors'* *'disposing'* of the native populations and pushing survivors to the west, where they survived as *'small dark'* peoples. That this could be written while the Holocaust was being enacted seems astonishing. However, the brutal truth is that the Beaker People did come from Europe, they did have a different culture and better weapons, and their DNA is in us all today.

This story's site is Fairy Knowe cairn, which was excavated in 1868 and found to contain a Beaker grave along with weapons and what appear to be animal sacrifices. So was this the grave of Stirling's first conquering invader, buried over the ground won at the edge of his sword? More recent analysis challenges our past assumptions. Yes there was migration, but—and it is a very big but—over what timescale, and was it just men? Was it over a year or two and was it all men seizing, as the Hawkes' put it *'the best pastures, and also no doubt their herds, and sometimes of their women'*? Recent DNA analysis confirms that the migrations took place over several generations and comprised men and women... perhaps refugees or gentrification and investment rather than invasion?

This site sits in a golf course, so please use caution and courtesy when approaching. We access it from the south through the University (NS 79593 98198).

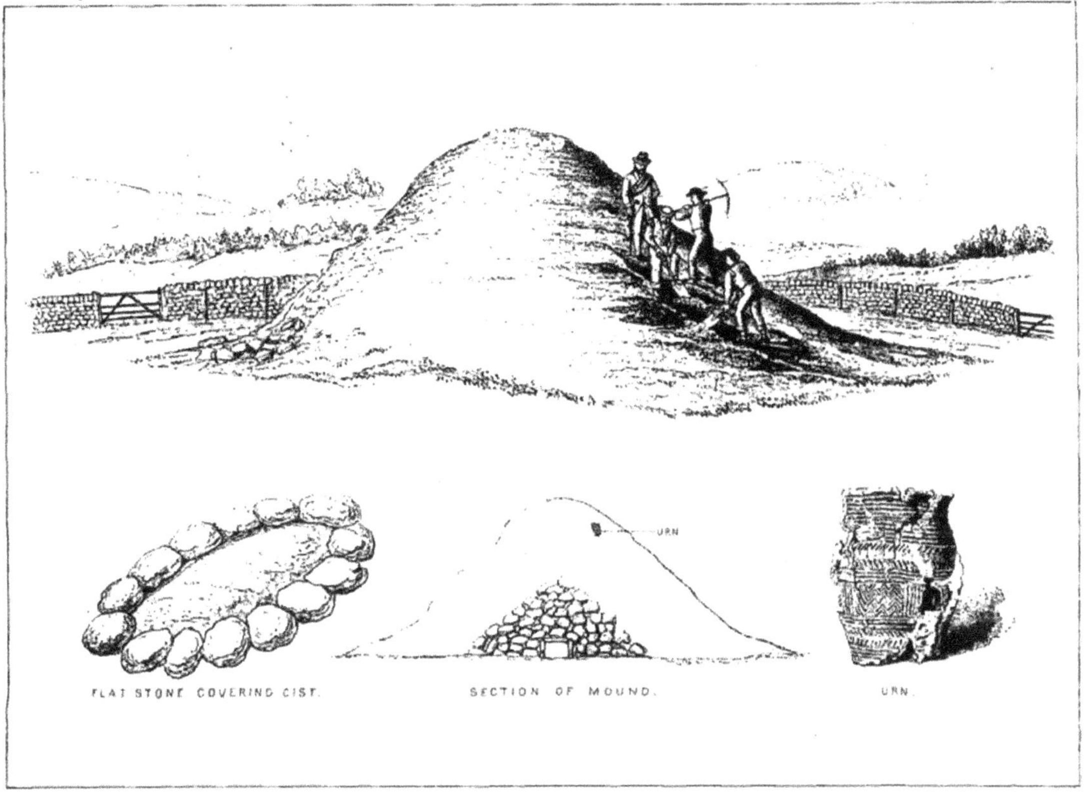
URN
FLAT STONE COVERING CIST.
SECTION OF MOUND.
URN.

W. & A. K. Johnston, Edinburgh. J. E. ALEXANDER, COL. DEL.

OPENING OF THE FAIRY KNOWE, PENDRICH.

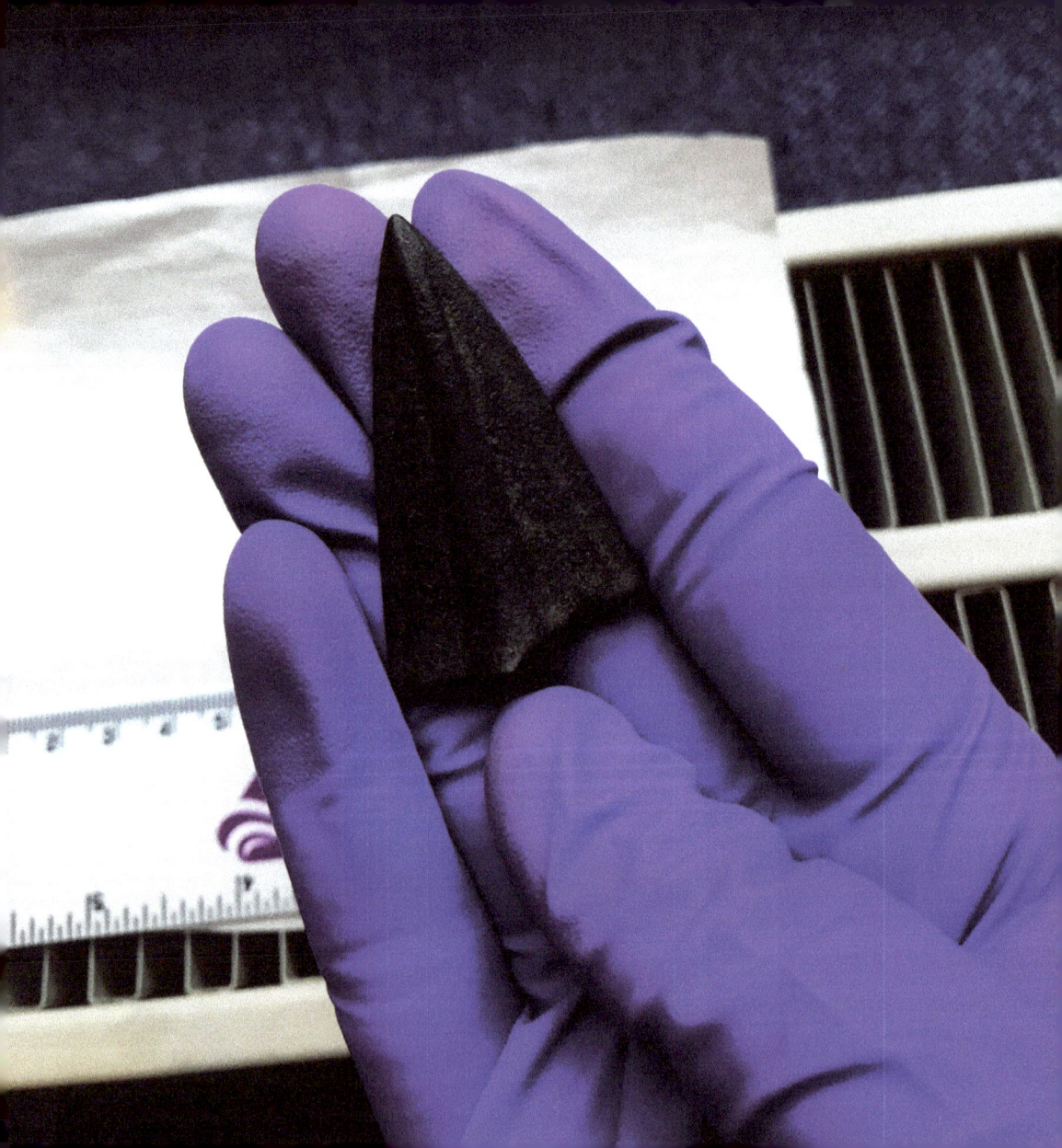

The Abbey Ford: Part 1

Stirling's First Act of Violence?

This little greenish pointy object is a 3,000 year old spear tip, and was recovered by SARG metal detecting club on the Abbey Ford during filming for the programme *River Hunters*. Now while arrows and axes have numerous other possible uses, we tend to think that Late Bronze Age spears were designed to be weapons of war. Our standard view is that after centuries of warm, pleasant weather, Scotland was becoming colder and wetter; farms were failing, and people began to move. Amongst these climate change-driven refugees, some will have found welcoming homes while others turned to raiding, which will have prompted a response in kind. During this period there was a literal arms race, with people developing ever more lethal types of weapon. Some of this likely reflects an elite that was obsessed with appearing war-like and martial, but clearly people were defending themselves and attacking others.

Abbey Ford is a remarkable location: perhaps the most important natural fording point in Scotland. A rocky outcrop exposed at low tide, it is the only point where crossing the Forth is possible dry shod. Metal detection revealed activity from c 2500 BC to c 1500 AD. Its importance declined as first the Roman ford at Drip (we will explore this later) was built, and then Stirling Bridge was constructed.

There are two key possible explanations for our broken spear tip. The first that it was thrust at someone crossing the ford and perhaps snapped between their ribs. The second that it was broken by its owner and thrown into the river to appease the gods… perhaps for a dry summer or successful raid. Again, we shall never know!

This location is Cambuskenneth Abbey (NS 80886 93909), and we do not recommend you venture onto the Abbey Ford as it is surrounded by metre deep mud and the tidal surge can be terrifying.

Leckie Broch
Destroyed in Shock and Awe?

Brochs are normally found in northern and western Scotland but there are a few around Stirling, all slightly later than their Highland cousins and all of them seem to have been lived in during the Roman occupation of Scotland. Leckie sits on a small rocky knoll, itself decorated with an array of much older rock art, which may have been why the broch was built there. These Stirling brochs appear to be built to control trade routes around Stirling's western carse: the large area of low-lying boggy ground that ensured the strategic significance of Stirling and its crossing points across the Forth.

Leckie contains a wide range of Roman goods including coins, drinking vessels and jewellery; perhaps bribes to pay for peace to allow trade across their lands? However, it seems likely that whatever arrangement existed came to a fiery end. The broch was partially dismantled and set on fire, and amongst the smouldering remains was uncovered a Roman ballista bolt (now in the Hunterian Museum in Glasgow). The excavator, Dr Euan Mackie, argued that the Roman army destroyed Leckie Broch, and Professor Bill Hanson has argued that this may have been a reprisal for resistance to the construction of the Antonine Wall. Another intriguing option is that perhaps the inhabitants destroyed it themselves after the abandonment of the Antonine Wall and the resultant shift of the Roman purchasing power to Northumbria, perhaps resulting in an economic collapse? However, it's also clear that the occupation continued at the site past the abandonment of the Antonine Wall, and perhaps even Emperor Septimius Severus's invasion when it was one of the surviving sites in the Forth valley.

There is no parking near Leckie broch (5.1 NS 69234 94018) and you have to walk from Gargunnock (5.2 NS 70300 94236) along the 18th century military road (where the Jacobites marched in 1745), which is very pleasant.

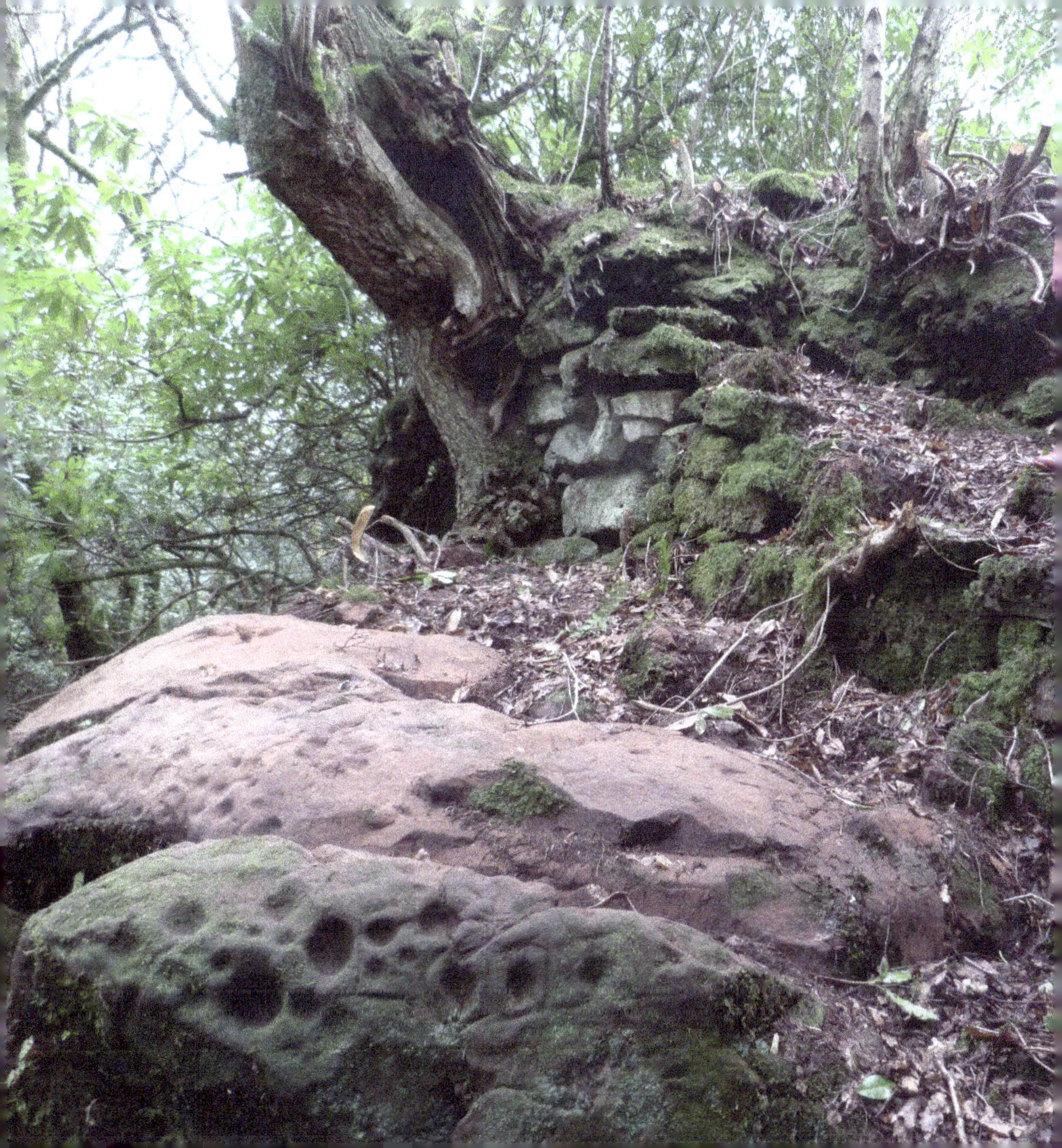

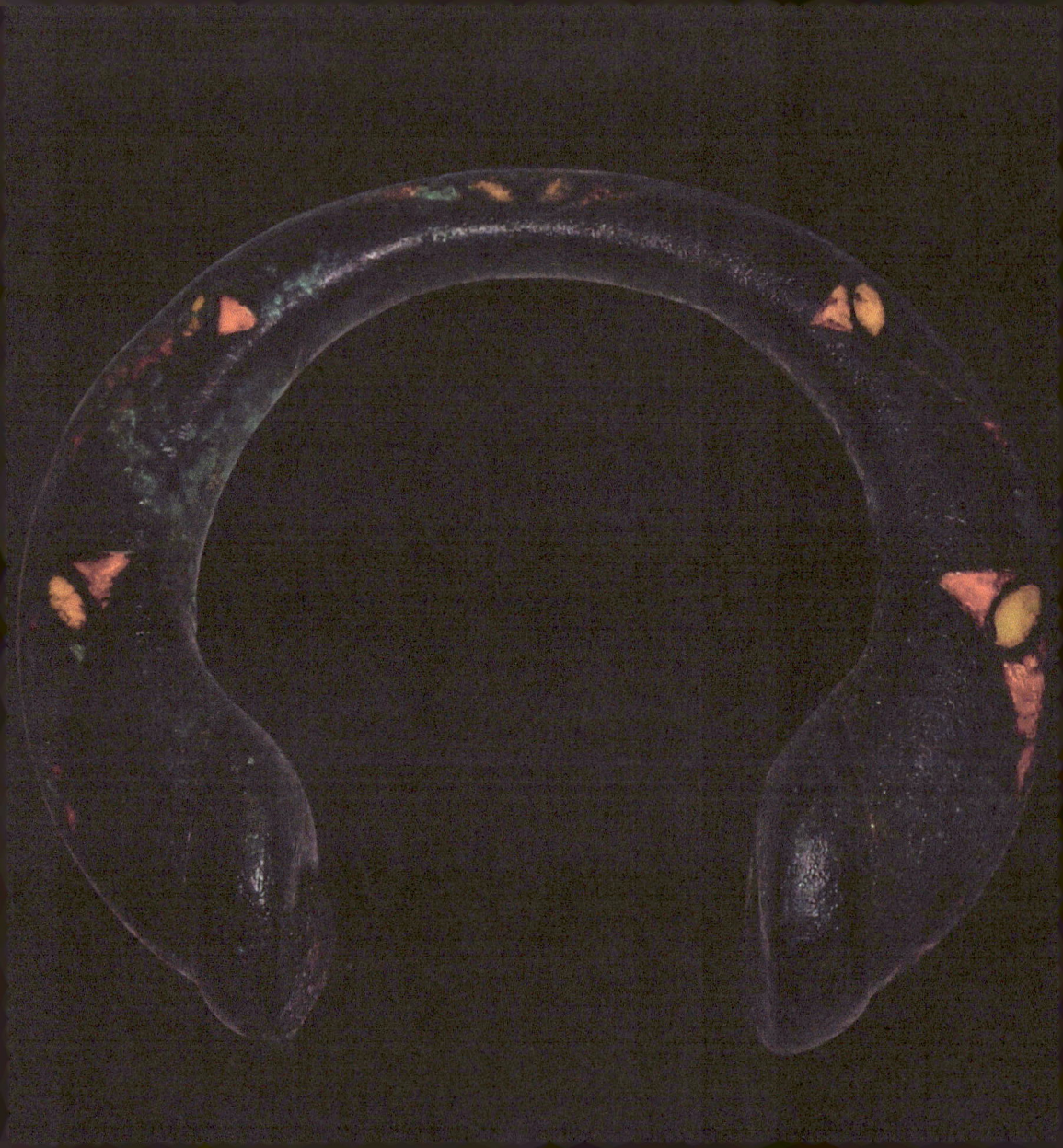

A Celtic War Chariot

In his biography of General Agricola, the historian Tacitus describes the battle of Mons Graupius between the deadly efficient Roman Legions and the doomed Caledonians. He describes them in chariots '*clattering in a wild display*' ahead of the fighting; a display of martial prowess by the aristocracy. While the location of the battle is unknown, the most likely location is called *Victoria* and marked on the second century Roman Ptolemaic map. It looks like Victoria is in Perthshire and, given that the battle is the culmination of the invasion, it seems likely that locals from Stirling fought in it and perhaps even drove their chariots north. However, there has always been some suspicion of Tacitus's description: why would anyone still be using chariots? It seems archaic, perhaps even an attempt to make the Caledonians seems wild and primitive.

It is at this point that local metal detectorist Alan George Baxter enters our story. On a misty spring morning in 2015 he started in another field, shivering as he got out of the car, ever hopeful that today would be the day! And indeed it was... he found two very precious items dating to the 1st or 2nd centuries AD, i.e. potentially contemporary with Mons Graupius: a terret ring for controlling a horse drawn chariot, and a tankard handle. These provide an incredibly rare insight into an elite warrior culture, where status was expressed through flash equipment and horsemanship, with the upper class warrior charging into battle behind their driver. Perhaps someone who had seen or even visited Leckie Broch? They were placed in a pit between Stirling and Falkirk. As these were fragments, is it even possible that they were recovered from the battlefield: tributes to the gods for a fallen warrior?

No location is given here, as the find is currently in Falkirk Museum.

Ardoch

The Best-Preserved Timber Roman Fort in the World

The point of Rome's invasions of Scotland was to turn our ancestors into good little consumers, buying things and paying taxes. Ardoch, with its vast sets of defences, was first built by General Agricola in the late first century AD and may indeed have been established prior to Mons Graupius. It's part of what we now call the Gask Ridge, and opinion is divided as to whether this was a frontier (in which case it was the first linear frontier in the Roman Empire) or merely a staging post for a further push. Regardless, it was abandoned within 5–7 years, only to be reoccupied during the Antonine invasion. It's this that resulted in so many barriers, as the later forts were built within the older ones!

The idea was that Ardoch, perhaps known by the Romans as Allauna (which gives the root of the Allan Water), would become a city with the fort at its core, like York or Carlisle or Chester. To the north of the fort is an extra-mural enclosure where the brave civilians who had followed the army into the wild barbaric Caledonia to make a new life were based. When Ardoch was abandoned again (after about 20 years), these poor people would've had a choice: to follow the army or to stay in their homes and risk the onslaught from the tribes to the north. One possible legacy of the occupation was literacy. The Greenloaning Stone (now in the garden of the Smith Museum of Stirling), from a nearby burial cairn, may feature a personal name in a Latin script (which we can't read yet). Did a legionary teach someone to read and write—and if so, what was their relationship?

We recommend you park to the west of the fort (NN 83828 10080) and access it from the north and walk through the Roman gateway. This, however, requires walking along the verge of a busy road. The safer option is to walk by the wee gate to the left of the estate entrance.

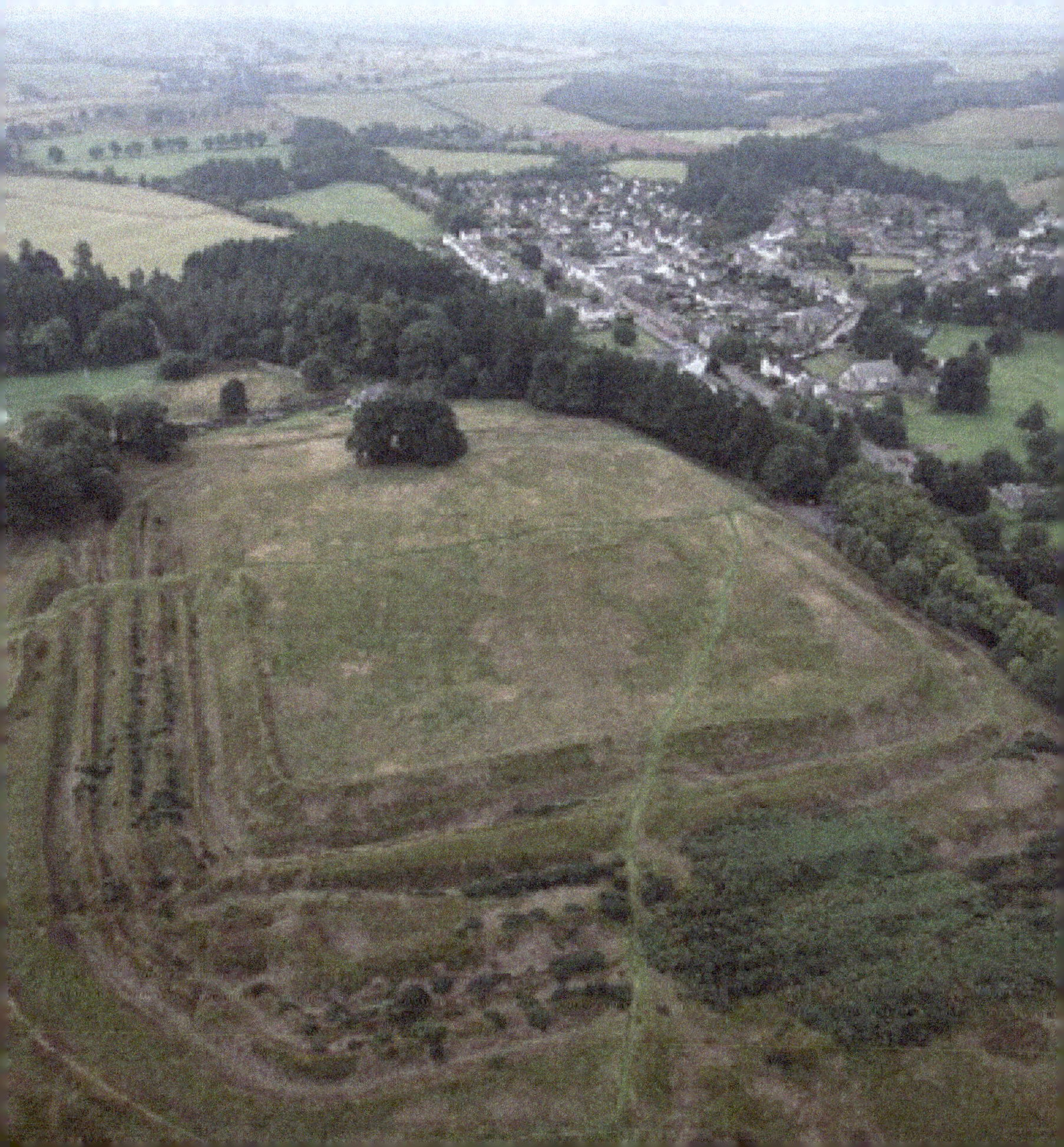

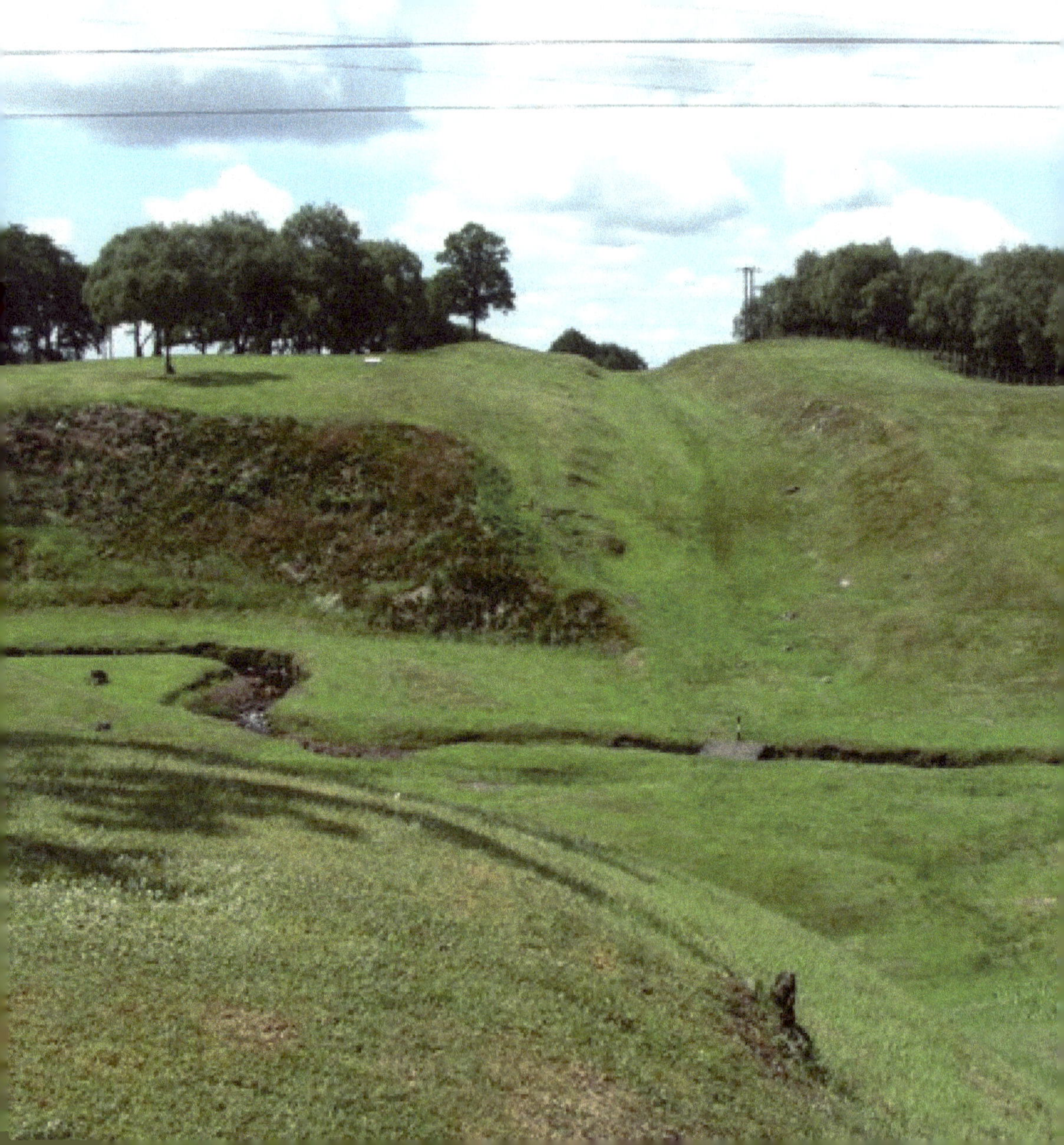

The Antonine Wall: Part 1
The Most Heavily-Guarded Frontier in the Roman World?

The 71 mile long Antonine Wall, constructed on the orders of the Roman Emperor, is often viewed as a political exercise to provide the newly-crowned ruler with a victory in the far, barbaric north. However, the risk of invasion was real (we heard about possible reprisals against Leckie Broch earlier), and the wall itself was redesigned midway through completion (145–50 AD) to increase its troop density. During its life, the wall required the same number of soldiers (6,000–7,000) as the twice-as-long Hadrian's Wall, making it one of most heavily-guarded fortifications in the Roman World. The wall was, in fact, not the frontier, which was north of the refortified Ardoch on the Gask Ridge.

It comprised a turf rampart on a stone base made of Roman army regulation size turves: 45 cm by 30 cm by 15 cm. To the south was a road, then a ditch. Between the rampart and the ditch was a berm which was lined with pits, which are assumed to have had spikes in them and are sometimes called lilia: the Latin for lillies. The ditch was generally 12m wide and 4m deep. Beyond the ditch was the stony upcast from its excavation, which often survives higher than the rampart (and is now often confused with the wall), and which acted as another barrier.

We advise parking at the Bonnyside (8.1 NS 83826 79799) on your way to Rough Castle (8.2 NS 84519 79875), which lets you walk along a good length of the wall past one of the signal platforms (8.3 NS 83791 79804).

The Antonine Wall: Part 2
Rough Castle - Its Best Excavated Fort!

The wall itself was built by three different legions, and it took around 1,730,000 man days to build. The most famous of them, Legio XX Valeria Victrix, likely built Rough Castle and fought at Mons Graupius, and were involved in Britain from the Claudian invasion to the end of Roman rule.

Rough Castle is the most completely excavated and displayed of the Wall's 17 forts and 8 fortlets, and had actually started as a fortlet until it was upgraded, also gaining an annexe and a bath house. Rough Castle also has another wee surprise: beyond the ditch upcast were a further line of 10 lillia, left open after excavation so you can recreate how hard it would be to cross at speed while under attack!

As so much of it survives, you can wander round its streets and imagine its buildings and the soldiers rushing to follow commands. In fact, we even know one of the people who barked orders in headquarters, who slept in a warm bed in the house, and who no doubt kept a watchful eye on the granary of the food supply. Flavius Betto of our friends the XXth, while on secondment as the acting commander of the Sixth Cohort of Nervians (from what's now northern France), erected an altar to Victory, which was found near the fort in 1843.

The end of the wall's use was definitely a political issue: there simply wasn't enough in Scotland to justify the military presence. We were too poor, too cold, and there was nothing to tax and steal! However, while Rough Castle was systematically demolished, there is evidence that Castlecary to the west was occupied for another 25 years in what would be a very lonely, isolated outpost!

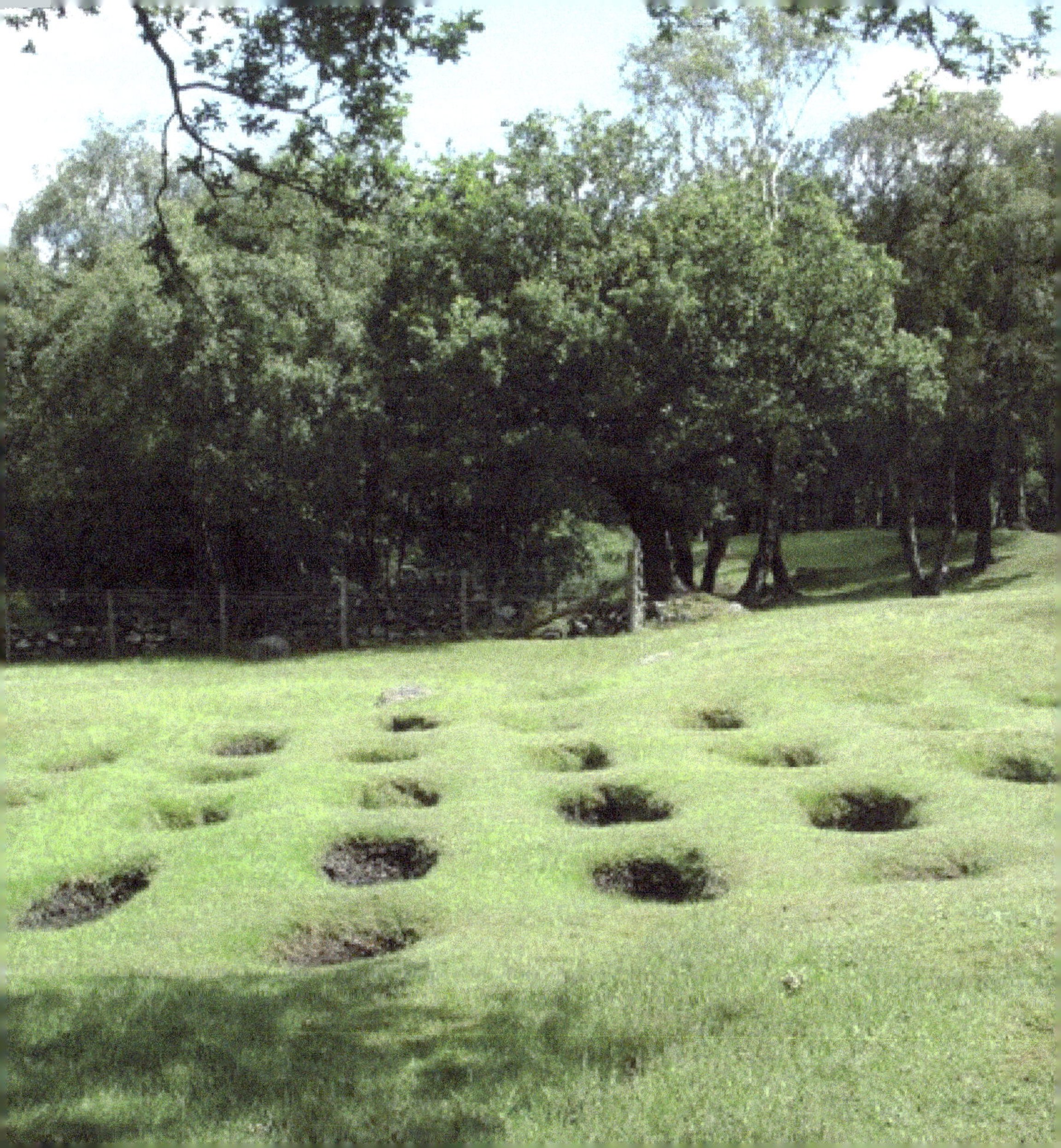

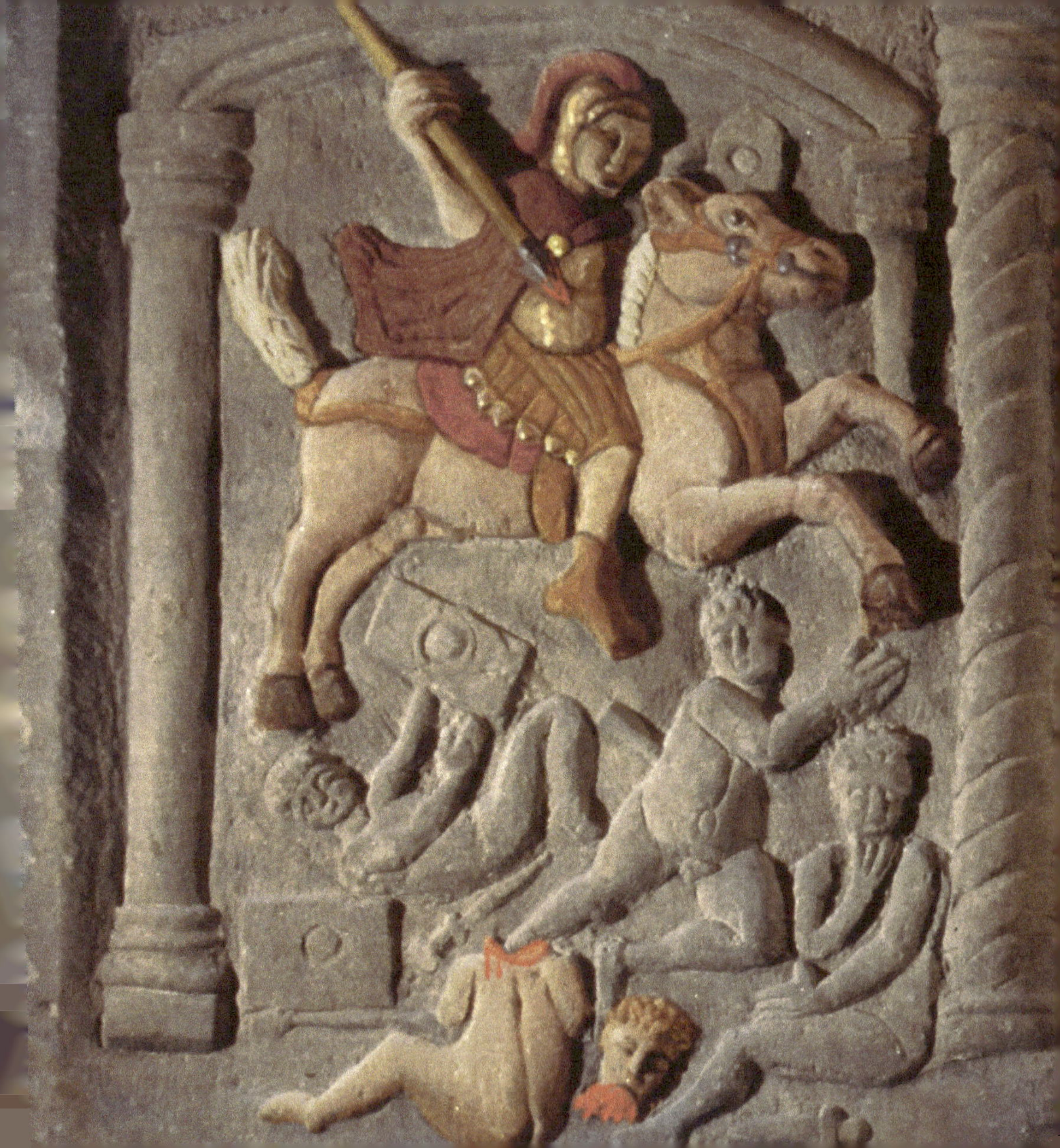

The Antonine Wall: Part 3
The Gruesome Bridgeness Slab

As the wall was built by different legions,[1] they were in competition with each other, and to record this they carved mile stones and monuments to chronicle their success and glorify the Empire. The biggest and best of these is the Bridgeness Slab from Bo'ness. The slab, along with most of the other monuments, had a ritual significance and had been carefully buried before the Roman retreat. Think of the lowering of the Union Jack at the handover ceremony of Hong Kong. The slabs are a uniquely well preserved celebration of both the empire's successes and ultimate failure.

The inscription reads *'For the Emperor Caesar Titus Aelius Hadrianus Antoninus Augustus Pius Father of his Country, the Second Augustan Legion completed [the Wall] over a distance of 4652 paces'*. The left panel shows a victorious Roman cavalryman with four naked[2] and much smaller defeated Britons. The right panel shows a suovetaurilia: a dedication ceremony conducted before campaigns, then probably the wall's construction. The man in the toga—possibly Aulus Claudius Charax, commander of the Second Legion—is depicted pouring a libation on an altar as a preliminary to sacrificing a bull, a pig and a sheep. The cries of distress from the animals were probably drowned out by the instruments.

The slab was originally painted, and the reconstruction by Dr Louisa Campbell is based on a detailed analysis of surviving pigments on the stone. A bloody symbol of oppression and defeat... perhaps a fate endured by the occupants of Leckie Broch or the Airth charioteer?

Ochtertyre Ford: Part 1
In the Footsteps of Emperors

The Roman Empire required reliable crossing points, and without a bridge over the Forth you must also cross the Teith. We think the Roman road crossed the Forth at Drip Ford (as we discuss later) and then headed towards the 1st century fort at Doune, part of the Gask Ridge. The construction of the road funnelled all subsequent invasions this way including Vikings, Edward I, Cromwell and Cumberland.

We know at least two Roman armies—each with thousands of legionaries—crossed at Ochtertyre, because of two temporary marching camps to either side of the Teith. These were used by the army for overnight stays after a day's march. The camp to the north has a small annexe which is argued to be associated with Emperor Septimius Severus and his family as they marched north with 50,000 troops around 210 AD. Given the status of the Emperor at this point, the camp was the *de facto* capitol of the Roman Empire, as power travelled with him.

Trouble had been brewing on this most barbaric northern frontier for some time. Around 180–82, Cassius Dio claims that the greatest war in the Empire was in Britain: that the Britons crossed *'the wall that separated them from the Roman legions, proceeded to do much mischief and cut down a general together with his troops'*. This was all suppressed within a few years, but by 197 we learn that the Caledonians (from Perthshire) were not keeping to the peace terms and were preparing to aid the Maeatae (who give their name to Dumyat: fort of the Maeatae). The Roman Governor Lupus was forced to buy peace, though he managed to secure the return of some captives—perhaps captured in 182? Is it possible that the prisoner exchange took place here... an Iron Age Check Point Charlie?

Access here is tricky as parking is limited, but we park to the north (11.1 NS 75980 97991) just to the south of the Severan marching camp³ and then walk down to the Teith (11.2 NS 75429 97920) and its various fording points along the road.

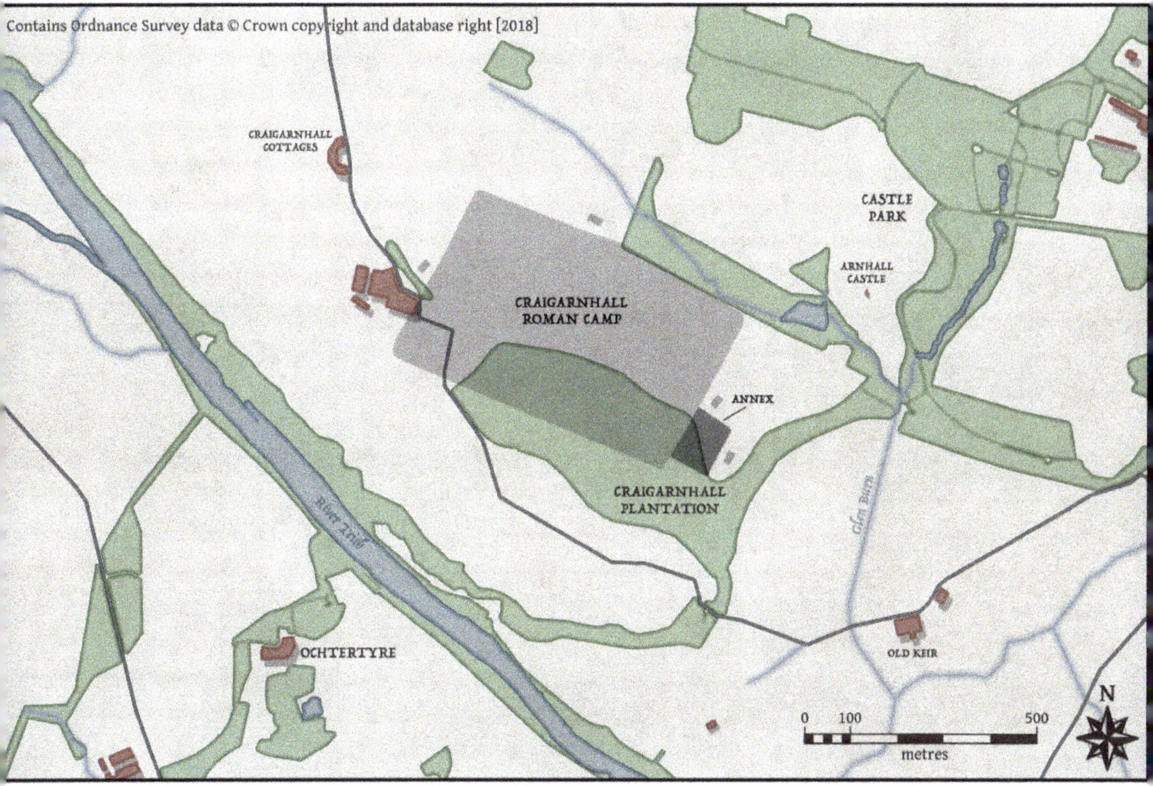

Contains Ordnance Survey data © Crown copyright and database right [2018]
CRAIGARNHALL COTTAGES
CASTLE PARK
ARNHALL CASTLE
CRAIGARNHALL ROMAN CAMP
ANNEX
CRAIGARNHALL PLANTATION
Glen Burn
OCHTERTYRE
OLD KEIR
N
0 100 500
metres

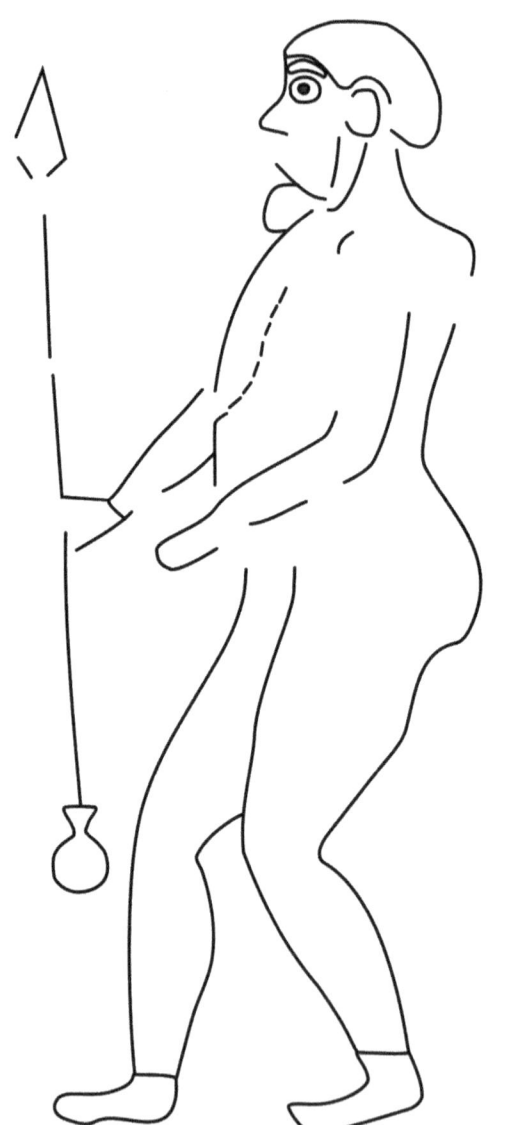

Ochtertyre Ford: Part 2
Septimius Severus' Enemy!

Within just over a decade the Romans were back, led by the Emperor. Silver had failed, so now it was time for steel. The locals fought a ferocious guerrilla campaign, and again they are described as fighting naked with chariots. Cassius Dio describes their weapons as '*a shield and a short spear, with a bronze apple attached to the end of the spear-shaft, so that when it is shaken it may clash and terrify the enemy*'. Now while this may be propaganda, there are depictions of naked warriors with spears with '*bronze apples*' at the base, like this example from Perth.

Septimius Severus won and agreed a peace with local chief Argentocoxos. After the treaty was signed, the Maeatae rebelled and Cassius Dio tells us that Severus '*summoned the soldiers and ordered them to invade the rebels' country, killing everybody they met; and he quoted these words from the* Iliad:

"*Let no one escape sheer destruction,*
No one our hands, not even the babe in the womb of the mother,
If it be male; let it nevertheless not escape sheer destruction".'

This was clearly an attempted genocide, but did it really happen? Well, the brothers managed to conclude another treaty, so there was clearly someone left alive. However, there is clear evidence for both a break in long-lived settlements, an absence of cereal pollen, and no more trouble from north of the Forth for nearly a century—so there was certainly some impact. However, when trouble returned it was far more serious... the Picts. The next hundred years marked raid after raid by the Picts, including the Barbarian Conspiracy of 367—many of whom will have crossed the Teith here. All of these incursions on the rich southern Roman provinces destabilised them, and the Roman state ultimately abandoned 'Britannia' around 410.

Drip Ford

Full of Pictish Corpses?

Drip Bridge, built in the late 18th century, replaced a ferry which had in turn replaced a ford described as '*a firm and solid bottom… little above two feet of water*'. This ford appears to have lain on the line of the Roman road constructed by Agricola and used by Antonine's troops and later still by Severus, and then all of those Picts raiding the Roman south.

This story focuses on the first rebellion of the Picts against the control of the invading Angles, and concerns the Battle of The Two Rivers in 671. The battle is described in the Life of St Wilfrith and describes a clash between a Pictish King, assumed to be Drest, and the Northumbrian King Ecgfrith. The battle took place between two rivers and so great was the Northumbrian victory that the rivers were blocked by Pictish corpses, and you could walk across them dry shod.

The location of the battle is unknown and several candidates have been suggested, but Drip—which sits next to both a meander in the Forth and the Teith's confluence—fits the evidence best as it lies on the assumed Roman Road which formed the likely route of the Northumbrian invasion. Gruesomely, if the fighting extended across the ford then it would not have taken too many corpses to walk dry shod across. The Picts would not endure the bitter taste of defeat for long and, in 685 at the Battle of Dunnichen, they pushed the Northumbrians to the Forth. The Picts and Northumbrians clashed twice more—an unnamed battle of 698, and finally The Battle of The Plain of Manau in 711 (between the Avon and the Carron)—and presumably the Roman road and ford at Drip was used each time. Did the Picts stop to remember their fallen comrades?

The location here is the late 18th century Drip Bridge, which likely sits next to the ford. Park to the west of the bridge (NS 76978 95600).

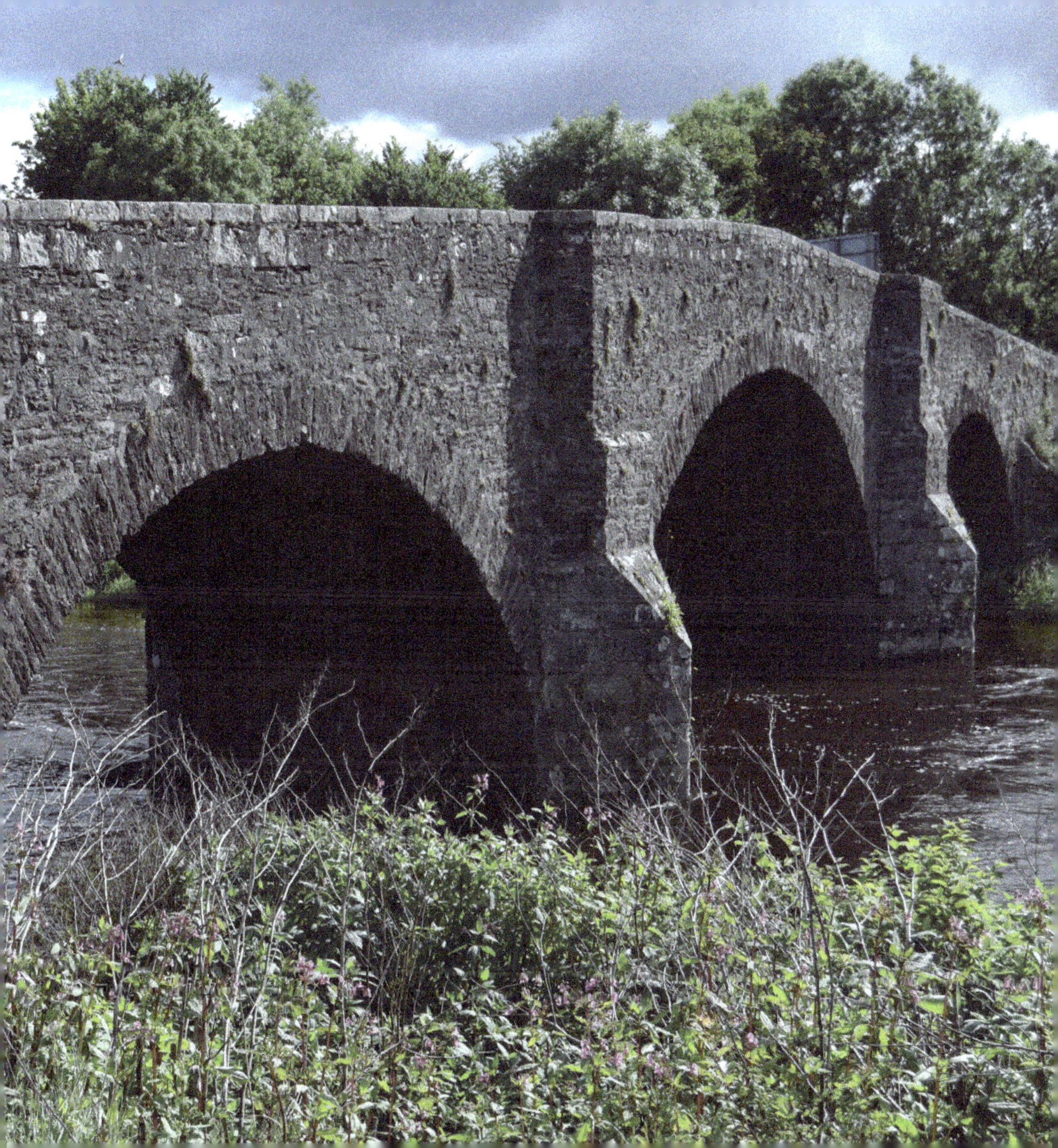

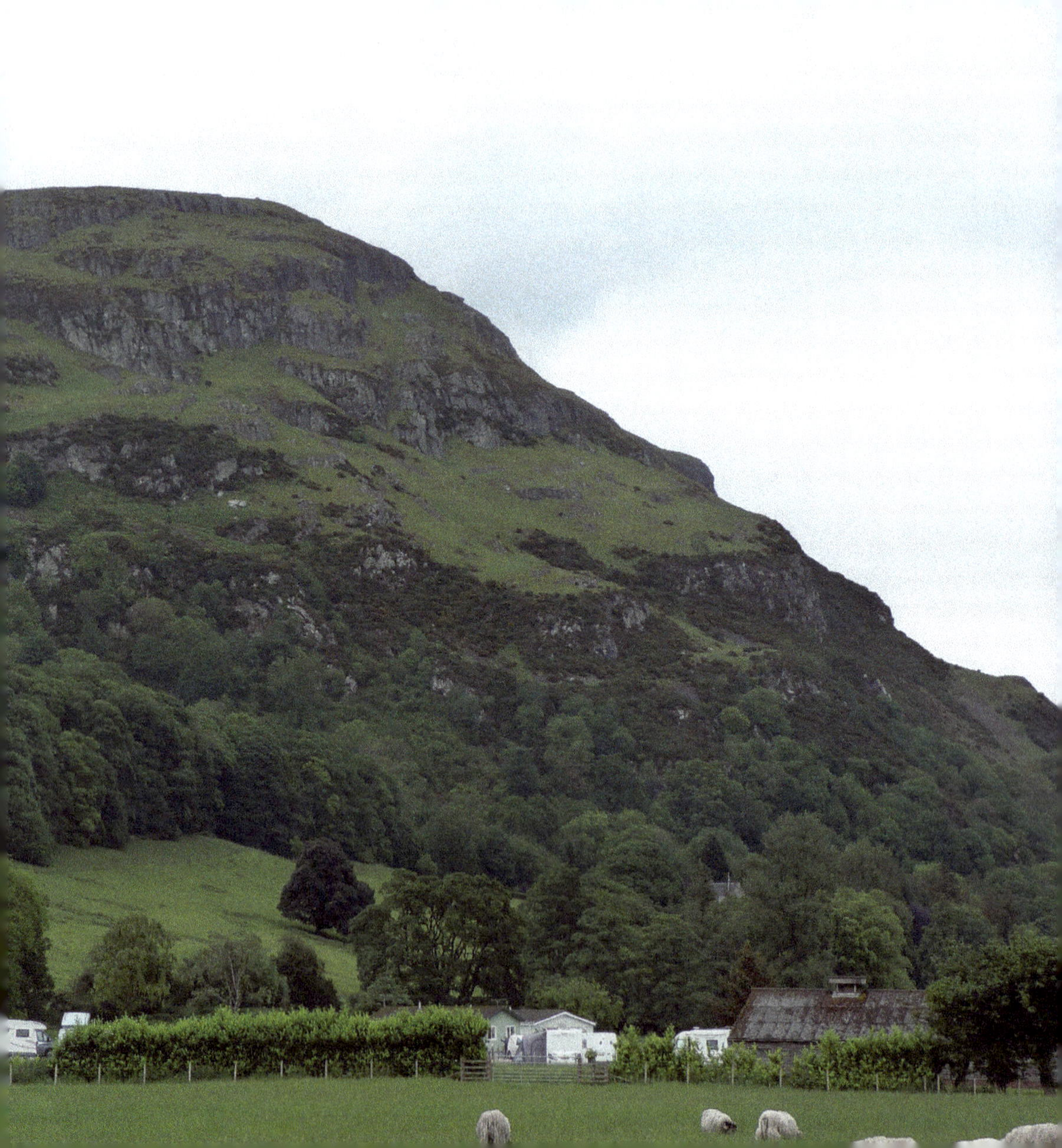

Dumyat

The Fort of the Maeatae, Capital of Manau

Stirling's ragged northern horizon is dominated by Dumyat: a low rounded lump of a hill above a 418m high cliff caused by a 400 million year old fault line. The Maeatae[4] were the local tribe who challenged Rome, but the actual fort (Castle Law 14.2 NS 83280 97364) is a little to the south-west: a smaller peak, but much more defendable. The Maeatae were also mentioned in *The Life of Columba*, and they lost a bloody conflict with a king of Dal Riata in the 580s. Dumyat is one of two Maeatae placenames, the other being Myot Hill in Falkirk. Clearly the Maeatae dominated the Forth crossings at Stirling. This would have been the jewel of Manau; perhaps the darkest of Scotland's lost kingdoms. It is first mentioned in Roman sources and lastly in the Battle of the Plain of Manau in 711. It gives its name to Clackmannan and Slamannan, but there are also Manau names in Balfron and West Lothian, and to the north it probably ran to the Earn.

A famous poem from around 600 AD, *The War Band's Return*, recounts a cattle raid on Manau from Galloway. The fort itself is vitrified, meaning its stone ramparts were set fire to and the scorching inferno reached such a high temperature that the stones melted and fused. An incredible statement of regime change, the smoke would be visible across the whole Forth Valley and the fiery eye of destruction even further at night. But who destroyed it? The Dal Riatans or the Angles... or perhaps even the Picts? Murray led the first excavation of the site and this indicated activity between the 5th to early 7th centuries, and this would fit any of them. Of course, to be fired the fort first had to be captured; can you imagine the nervous defenders watching the slow steady arrival of attackers, and their sheer terror when the gates fell and the enemy swarmed over hearth and home?

There are numerous ways up and down Dumyat, but most people in Stirling come from the west where there is a large, if informal, area of parking (14.1 NS 81305 98250) and a good path. It takes between 40 minutes and an hour, depending on your fitness.

The Abbey Craig
A Viking Stronghold?

The Abbey Craig is, of course, more famous as the home of the National Wallace Monument: the largest memorial to an individual in Britain. But round its base are traces of a double rampart system which, like Dumyat, was destroyed by fire and subsequently vitrified. The radiocarbon dates indicate that it was destroyed in the 7th to 10th centuries AD. This is contemporary with post Dunnichen settlement when the Pictish border with the Northumbrians became the Forth, so perhaps it was built to defend the frontier and destroyed in an Anglian raid? Another option is the Battle of Dollar in 875 when Danish Vikings led by Thorstein defeated the King of Picts Constantine I, who died two years later fighting another Norse invasion. It's likely that the Great Army had marched north, perhaps over the Drip or Abbey Fords. After Dollar, the Vikings rampaged for a year and may even have built some permanent settlement. So might the fort have been built to defend against Viking raids… or perhaps even built by the Vikings to control their newly carved-out sword land?

There are certainly local indications of Viking settlement: Logie Old Kirk, just to the north of Abbey Craig, contains fragments of up to four hogbacks which—while not Viking burial monuments—are likely to have been used by the children or grandchildren of Vikings. One of these two complete hogbacks lies north to south, while the other lies east to west, according to Christian tradition, and may reflect the conversion of the Vikings to Christianity. It is likely that there was a small, short-lived and unrecorded Viking kingdom centred on Abbey Craig that no doubt used the Forth to raid both north and south. These raids ultimately destabilised Pictland to such an extent that it rebranded itself with an Irish Dal Riatan identity as Alba.

The Abbey Craig is perhaps the most easily accessible hillfort in Britain; there is free parking (NS 80796 95771) and nice paved road all the way up!

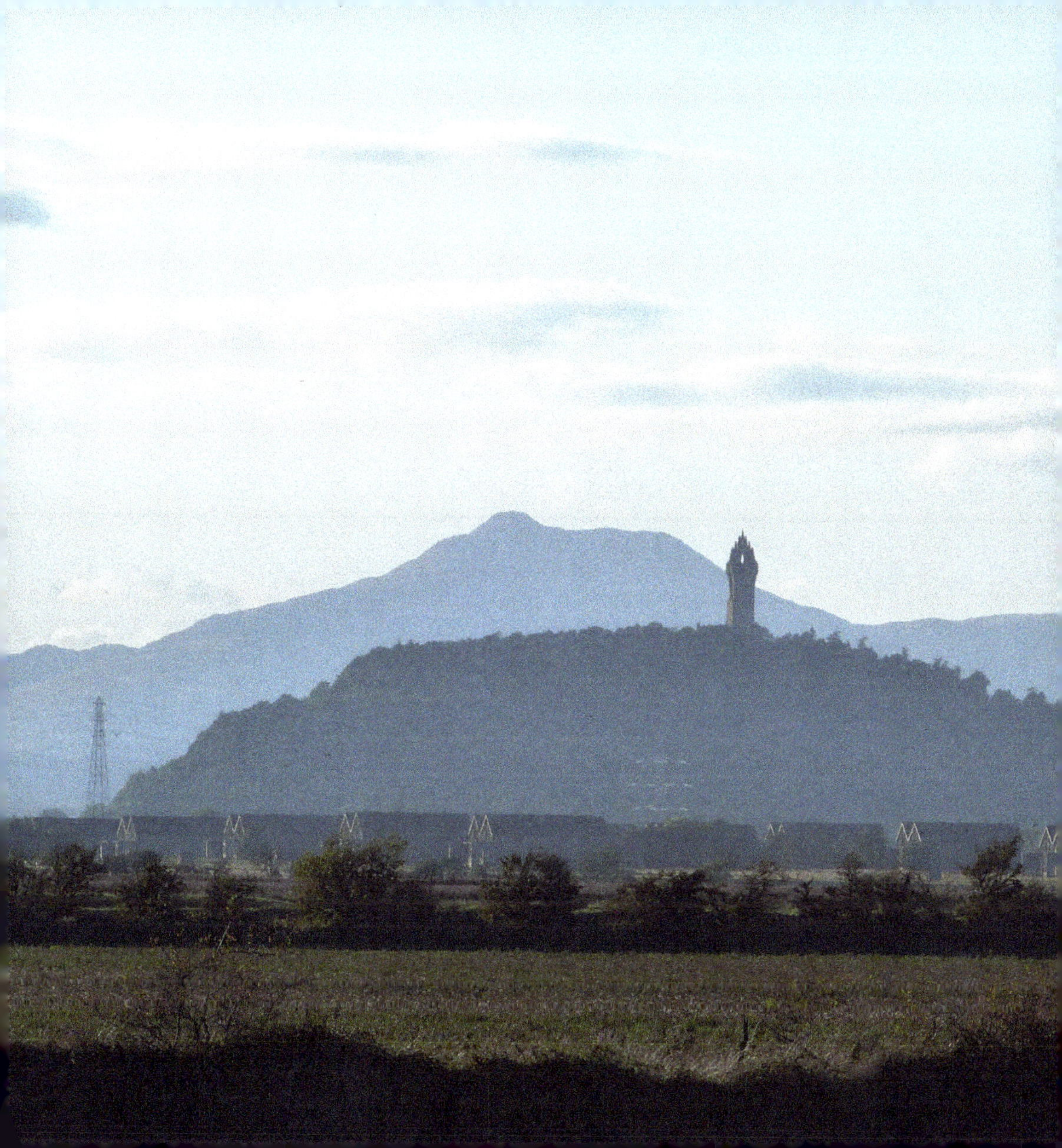

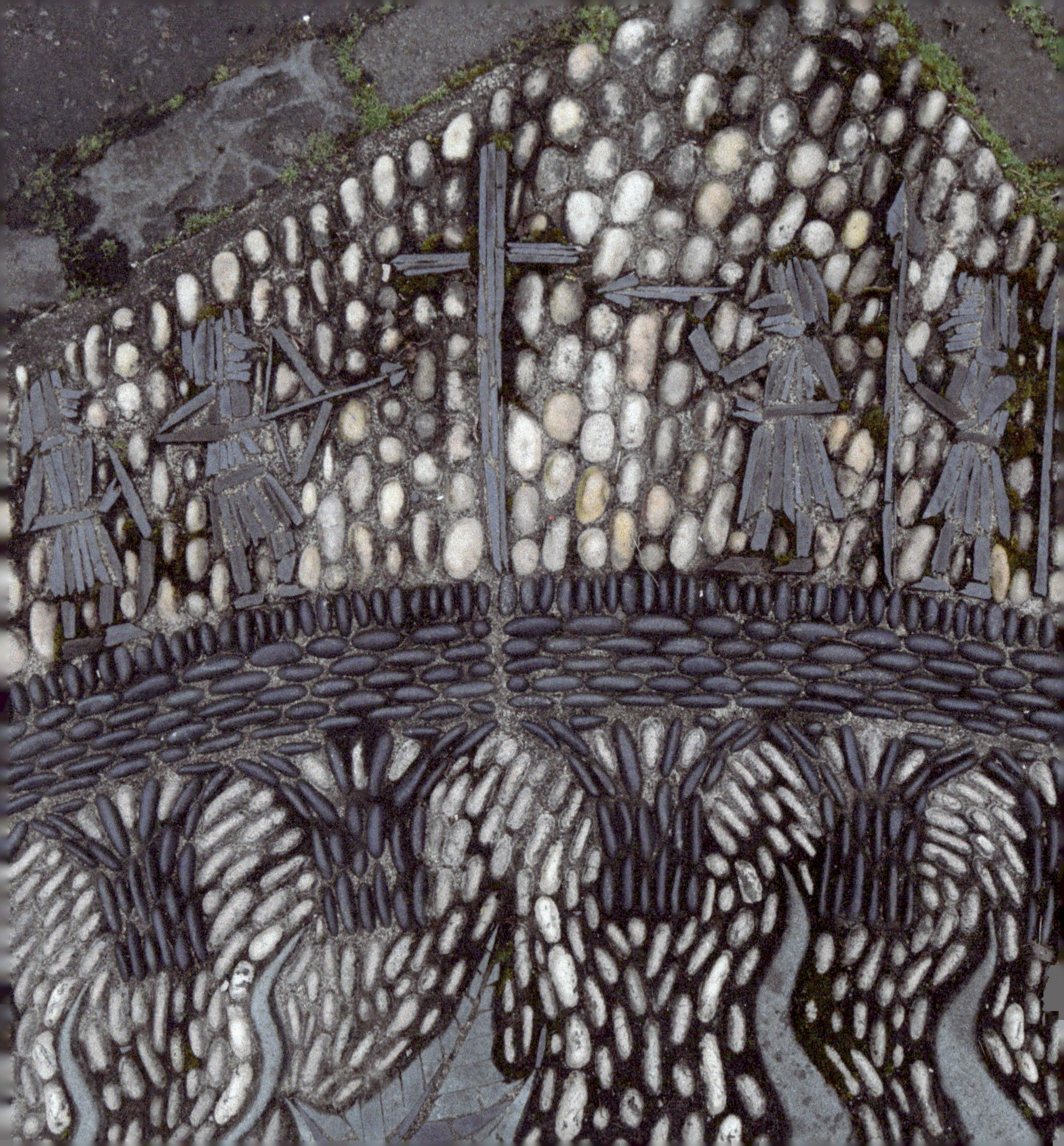

Stirling Bridge: Part 1

The First Bridge

As we have heard, the frontier between Pictland/Alba and the southern Kingdom of Northumbria was the Forth, with perhaps a little land bridge extending to the line of the Antonine Wall, some 10 miles south. All of this changed with Malcolm III, his wife the future St Margaret, and their children Edgar, Alexander and David—kings one and all. They pushed Alba's frontier's south, and one of them built the first bridge over the Forth.

Now Malcolm was a fighter, not a builder; Edgar may have built the first castle, but it's first recorded in Alexander's reign and indeed he died there. A bridge could not be built until you could be confident that it would not be used to aid invasion—as Wallace would discover, the Forth is a generous ally. Indeed, in William the Conqueror's invasion of 1072 he used the ford at Drip (as explained earlier). Murray believes that David built the bridge along with a vast investment programme in Stirling because of a very particular set of circumstances: he was never meant to be King.

David was called the Prince of the Cumbrians (Strathclyde Britons), and ruled a semi-independent zone between Alba and Northumberland including Strathclyde, Galloway, the Borders and the Lothians. The unexpected deaths of his elder brothers without legitimate heirs meant that David combined his substantial personal holdings with Alba, pushing the frontier from the Forth to the Tweed. Stirling was now secure; he could invest in it to boost its economy, it was granted burgh status and gained a high school and an Abbey. Cambuskenneth Abbey lies on the Abbey Ford, and it made no sense for David to have granted such a key asset unless he had already built a bridge which we think is depicted in the burgh seal. This seal reflects a complex society and an emerging sense of Scotland: conquering Scots and native Britons hostile but unified as Christians 'protected by the Cross'.

Parking here is easy (but the north side is quieter (NS 79772 94605), to spot the old bridge's location look up stream from the centre of the current old bridge.

Stirling Bridge: Part 2
Wallace and the Friar

Prior to the actual fighting at the Battle of Stirling Bridge an attempt at peace was made, hosted by some respected neutral parties: Dominican Friars from the Priory. You of course all know that peace was rejected and the fighting began. But it's worth spending a little bit of time on the Priory itself, a portion of which was excavated prior to the construction of new flats and was located at the bottom of today's Friar's Street: Stirling's Blackfriars. We have no images of the complex, but it must have been impressive as both Edward I and Robert the Bruce stayed there (though not together!). The excavation uncovered a single burial: a young man buried with a belt whose buckle survived, almost certainly showing that he was a friar. Radiocarbon dating indicated he was alive during the Wars of Independence. Given where he was buried and the time of his death, he could well have been a witness to the key events round Stirling: Stirling Bridge, the 1304 siege of Stirling Castle, and of course Bannockburn. He may well have saw, met or spoken to Wallace, Edward I and Bruce.

It's always tempting to envy people who had such a front row seat on the conflicts that shaped our country, but it must have been terrifying. It's also worth noting just how long they lasted: 1296 (The Battle of Dunbar) to 1328 (The Treaty of Edinburgh)—32 years, a whole generation who knew nothing but war. It was therefore appropriate to ensure that this long-gone friar was reburied with all the honour that Stirling could muster. His reburial in 2020 was conducted by his living brother Dominicans, and his final resting place is under Stirling Castle in Snowden Cemetery (17.2 NS 79074 93880).

From the bridge it's a short walk to the location of Stirling's Medieval Dominican Priory (17.1 NS 79698 93555).

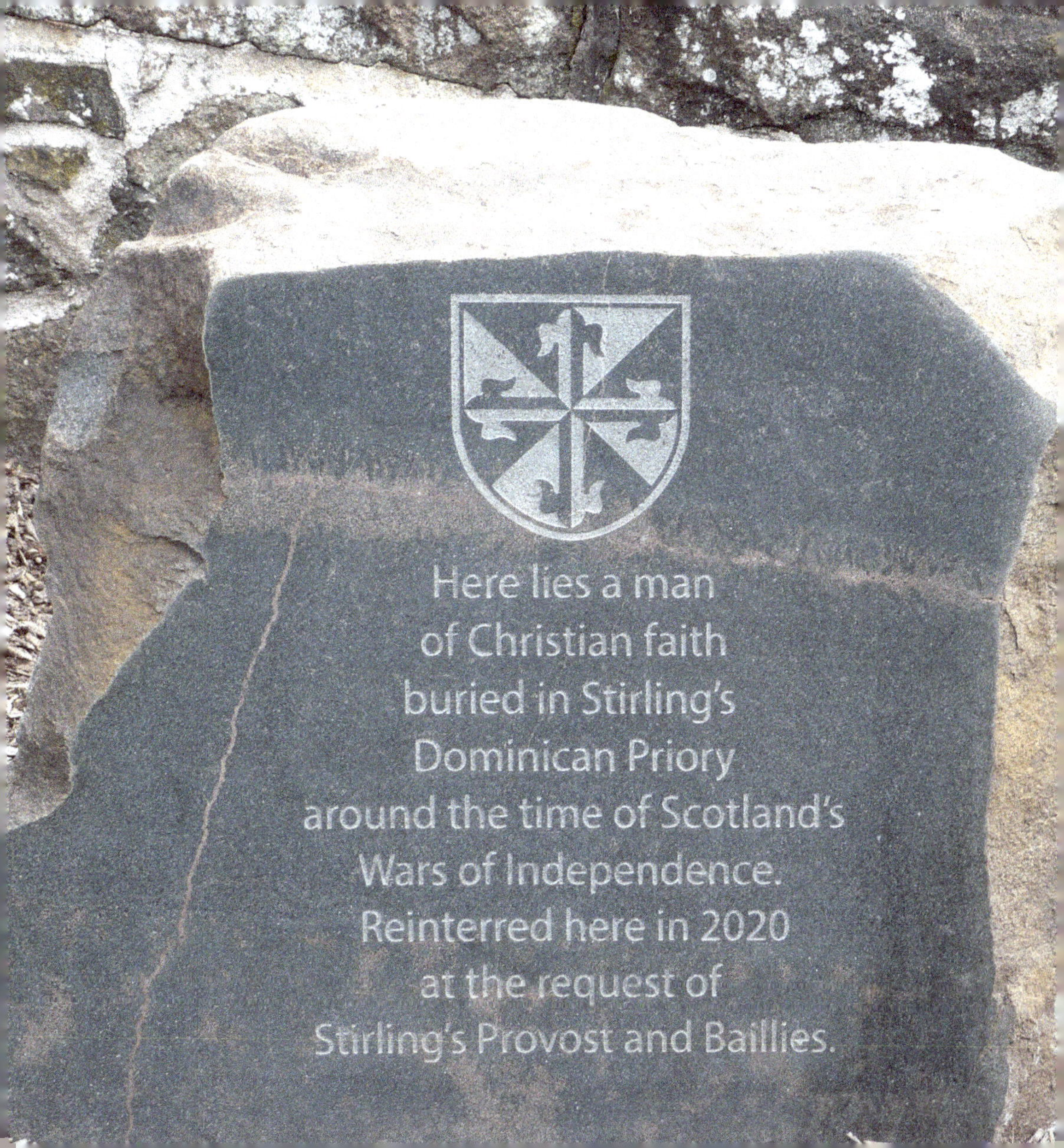
Here lies a man
of Christian faith
buried in Stirling's
Dominican Priory
around the time of Scotland's
Wars of Independence.
Reinterred here in 2020
at the request of
Stirling's Provost and Baillies.

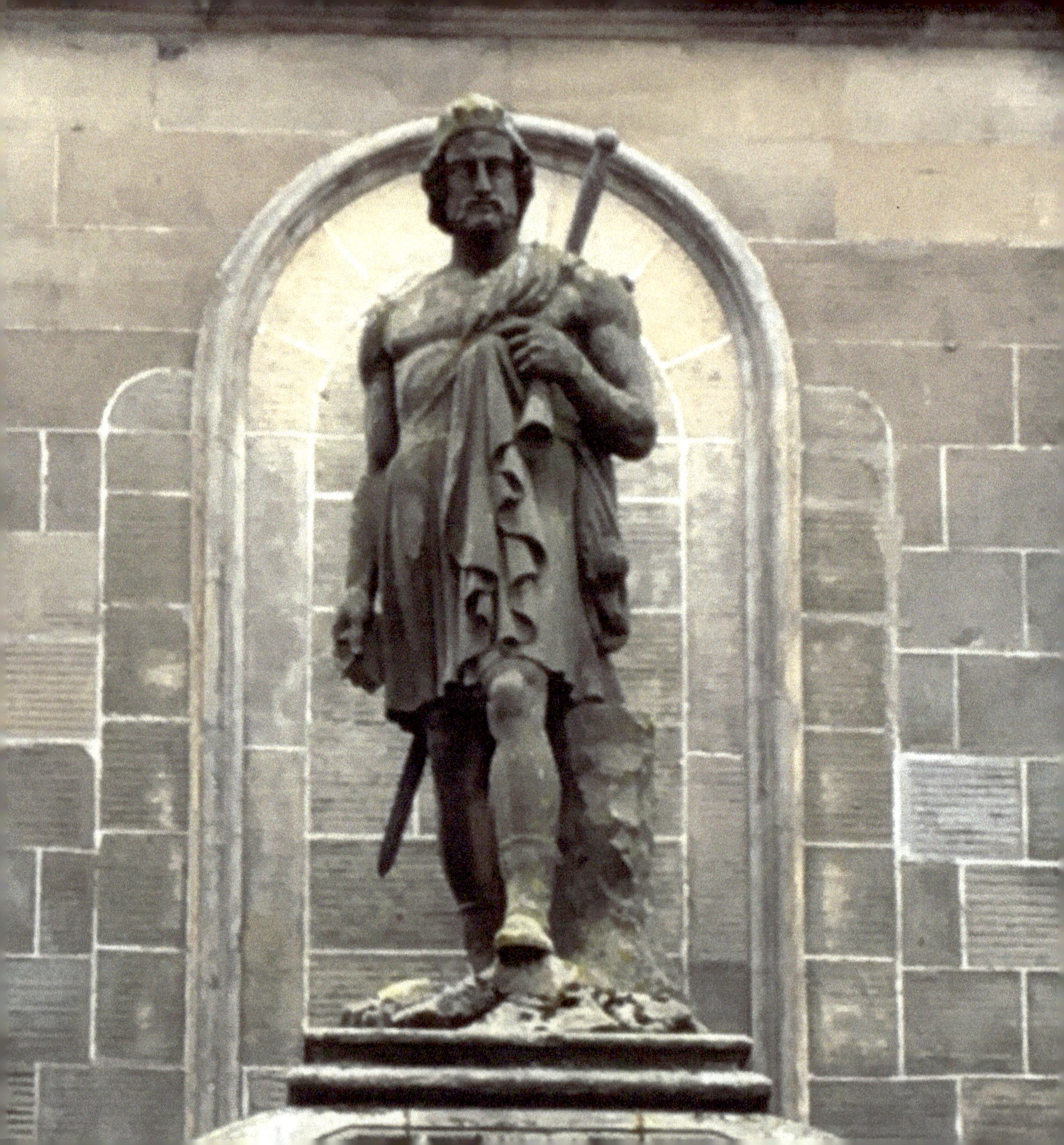

Stirling Bridge: Part 3

Sir William Wallace and the Bridge's Fiery Destruction

The key to Wallace's victory at the Battle of Stirling Bridge was English ignorance of the topography; first the bridge restricted troop mobilisation (though not perhaps as much as is claimed), and then there may have been a rising tide. However, it is clear that Wallace did not booby trap the bridge as the English troops crossed, as was claimed by Blind Harry the medieval poet who wrote an epic poem about Wallace. We know this because an English knight, Sir Marmaduke de Thweng, Keeper of Stirling Castle (who would personally surrender to Bruce at Bannockburn), retreated across the bridge riding on horseback through his own men. Now he would only have done this if the battle was going badly—and, of course, the bridge was still up for him to have ridden across.

The English records are quite clear: they destroyed the bridge to protect their rear. Its loss, and indeed the eventual destruction of the castle by Bruce after the Battle of Bannockburn—along with decades of conflict—had a dramatic impact on Stirling's economy, which dropped by 60% over the conflict. Just as with the Picts and the Northumbrians, Stirling became a frontier zone again.

The 1304 Siege of Stirling Castle: Part 1
The Brave Sir William Oliphant

Following the victory at Stirling Bridge, the Scots regained Stirling Castle only to abandon it again after the Battle of Falkirk. However, it was recaptured again in 1399 and was held by the brave Sir William Oliphant with between 120 and 25 defenders. Edward I took his time, and by 1304 he was ready to mount the most famous of Stirling Castle's many bloody sieges.

In addition to his own troops he also demanded support from his Scottish followers, who at this point included both Bruce (although Bruce was actively plotting against him) and the Red Comyn. Both had signed a treaty that required Wallace's head as the price of peace, though it would take nearly a year to catch him. He was also maintaining a watch on Drip Ford in case of Scottish reinforcements. That was still not enough, so Edward ordered Scottish churches to strip their roofs of lead and that all of '*Glasgow's iron as well as great stones and other material from Brechin, Dunfermline and St Andrew's be brought to him*' to make his siege engines.

The siege began on the 22nd of April 1304, and Edward built a platform for his Queen to watch it from, to show her the full impact of his mighty efforts: perhaps the most siege engines ever assembled by the English army. Edward asked if Sir William would surrender and, when he refused, it began. Thirteen catapults hurled projectiles at the castle day and night, for days, then weeks, and then months. Incredibly, not only did Sir William hold out but he also led a number of counter attacks with Scottish artillery and crossbows, narrowly missing killing Edward I twice and '*making a great slaughter of the king's army*'. But the siege was only going in one direction.

As Bruce destroyed most of the original castle it's not clear where Edward's army was placed, and either Ladies Rock (NS 79098 93777) or the Castle Esplanade are the most likely candidates.

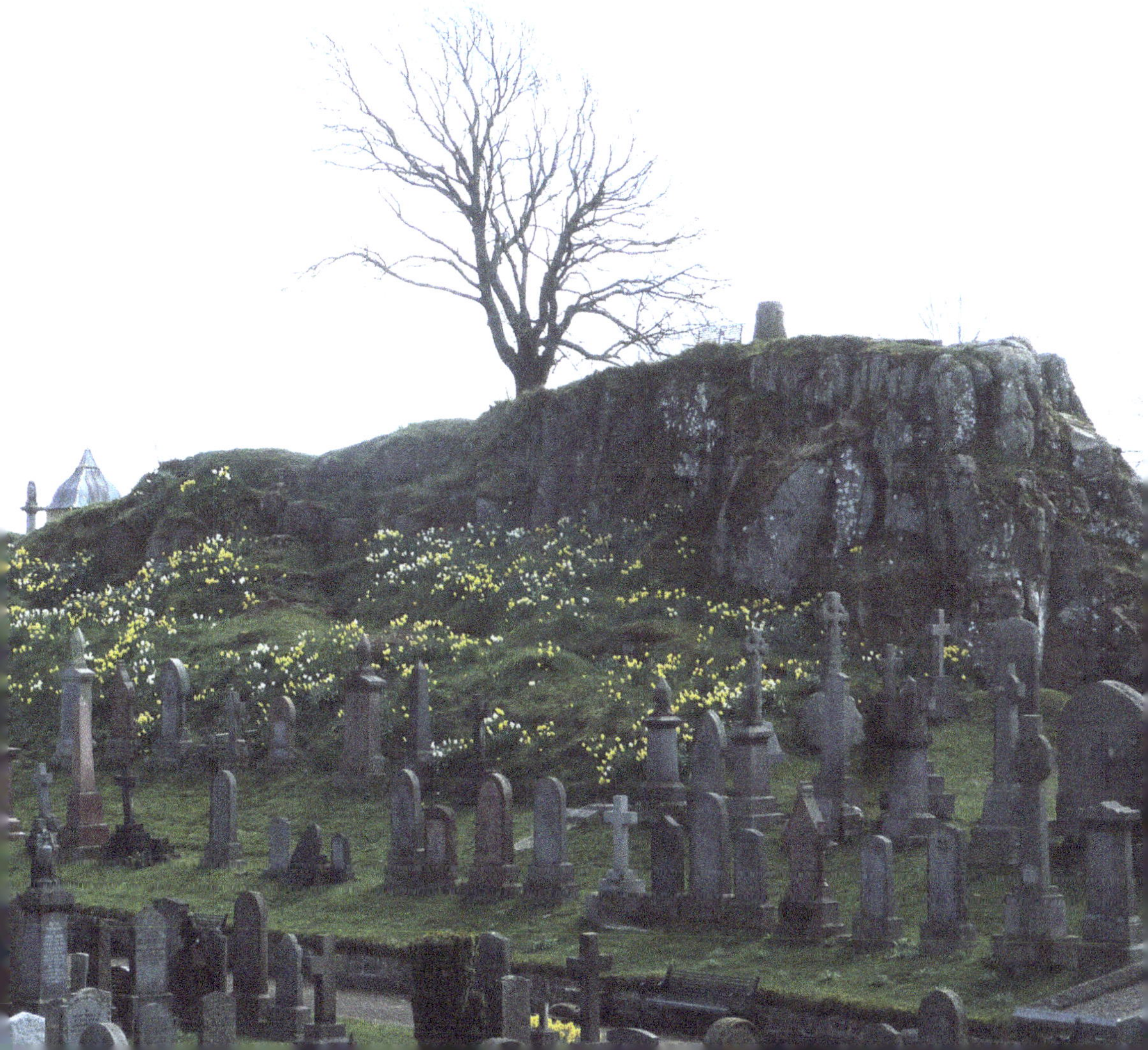

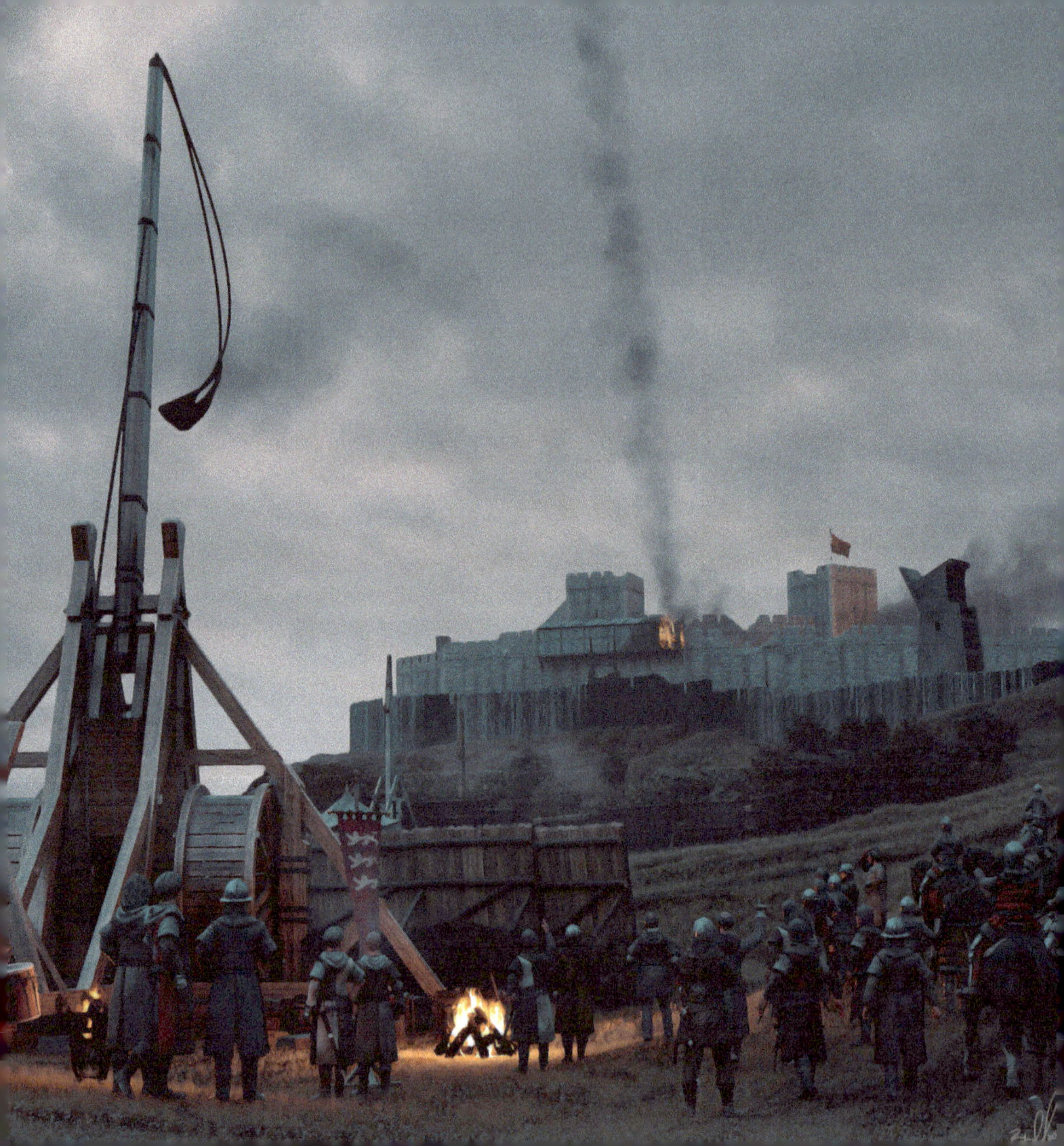

The 1304 Siege of Stirling Castle: Part 2
The War Wolf

After three months the food was inevitably running short and so, with honour served and no doubt suffering shell shock, Sir William offered to surrender on the 20th of July. Astonishingly—and in another indication of his dark nature—Edward I refused. He had tasked five master carpenters and 50 workmen to build what may have been the largest trebuchet ever built—the *loup-de-guerre*, or War Wolf[5]—and was keen to see it in action. He probably deployed it in the flat area of the cemetery, near the current statue of John Knox, and bombarded the castle from there. It was only when an entire wall of the castle had been destroyed four days later that Edward I let Sir William surrender. He made them leave in bare feet, with ash on their heads, before throwing themselves at his feet. Edward I had threatened to have them hanged and disembowelled, and it was only the intervention of his Queen that saved them.

We searched, in vain, to find some poetry to describe this incredible siege and the heroic actions of Sir William and his brave defenders, though I did find a pipe tune by Willie McColl. However, we suspect the reason Sir William is not more celebrated is that the siege may have broken him. As you know, within a year of his own surrender, Wallace had been executed—Scotland was crushed. Sir William wound up locked in the Tower of London, and was only released when he pledged allegiance to Edward I. Ironically, by 1312, he ended up in charge of Perth on Edward I's behalf, when it was subject to a failed six week siege by Bruce, who eventually captured the town by sneaking over the walls. Brave Sir William was captured and sent in chains to the Western Isles, where he later died; a very sorry end for one of Scotland's bravest heroes.

Milton Ford

The Last Fatal Charge of Brave de Bohun

As we heard, the first Scottish Wars of Independence lasted for 32 years. Thus Bannockburn in 1314 sits nearly in the middle and was not by any means the end of it. As you will find out, the battle took place over two days, and Day 1 was a rather small affair—no more than a bloody nose for the English. However, it took the Scots months of planning and training, as well as fighting all day, to win this meagre victory. Whatever comes to mind when you think of The Battle of Bannockburn is all to do with Day 2.

This story concerns the first casualty, and that day's fastest Englishman on horseback: Sir Henry de Bohun. As you will know, the Scots were besieging Stirling Castle and had given Edward II till mid-summer to come to the aid of his allies; to not do so would've been a major loss of face. So Bruce knew when and where the English were coming, and constructed pits like those at Rough Castle to restrict the English troops' movement. The plan was to stop them travelling to the castle by the main route (the old Roman Road) and force them onto the low-lying Carse between the Pelstream and the Bannockburn.

The Scots faced the English vanguard while the bulk of the army rested. As Bruce, mounted on a small horse, was giving one final morale-boosting rally, some English charged across the narrow ford and the quick de Bohun got ahead of the pack, catching Bruce unawares. Now this presented Bruce with a dilemma: to scuttle back to the Scots line would lose face and morale, but to stand was to risk death and disaster. The Scots' cause would fail on that muddy field. So Bruce calmly turned and faced the charging knight... catching him in a fatal, skull-crushing blow that split his favourite axe!

There is lots of free parking in Milton (21.1 NS 80092 89974), and the ford (21.2 NS 80292 89889) is short walk.

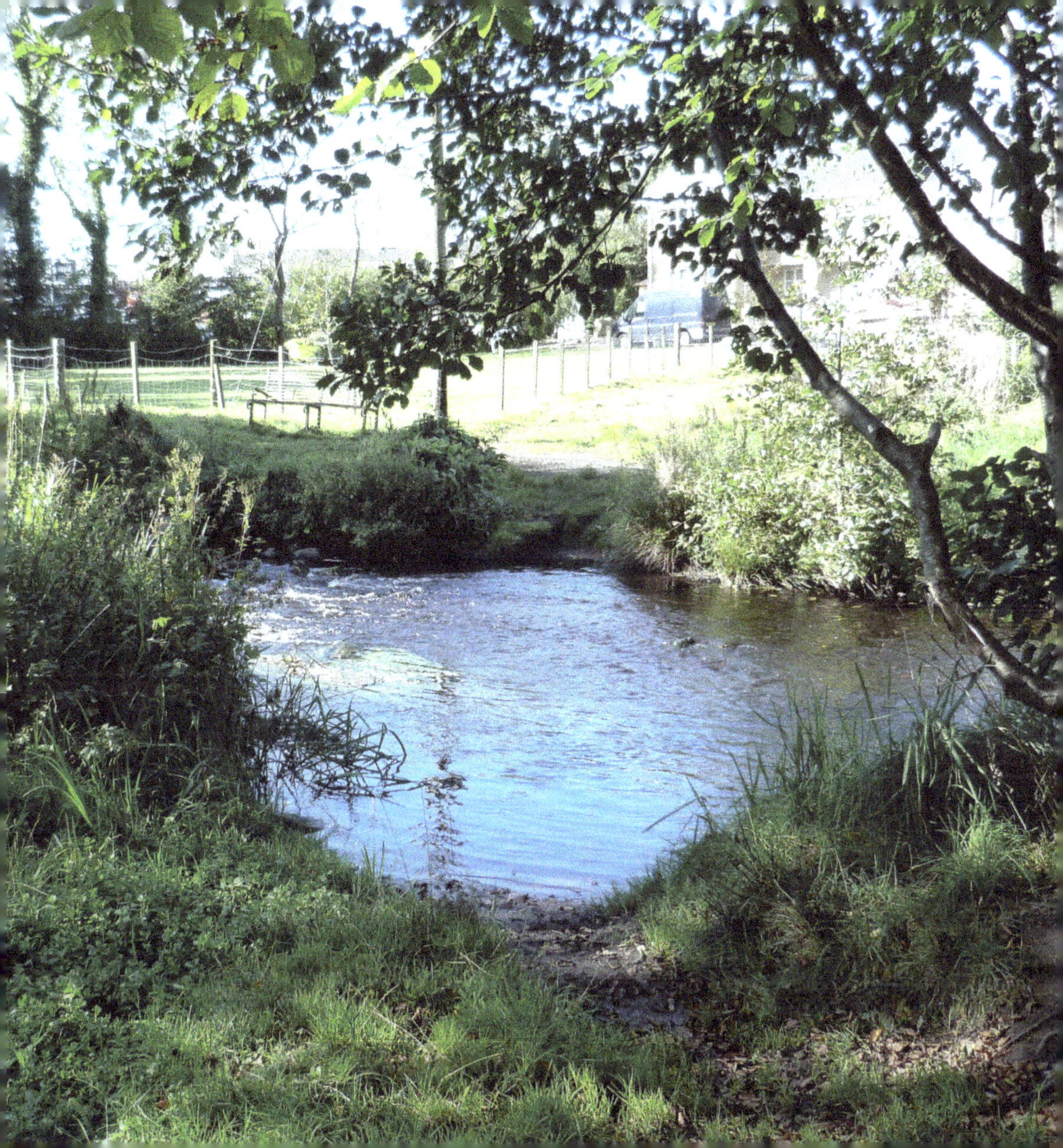

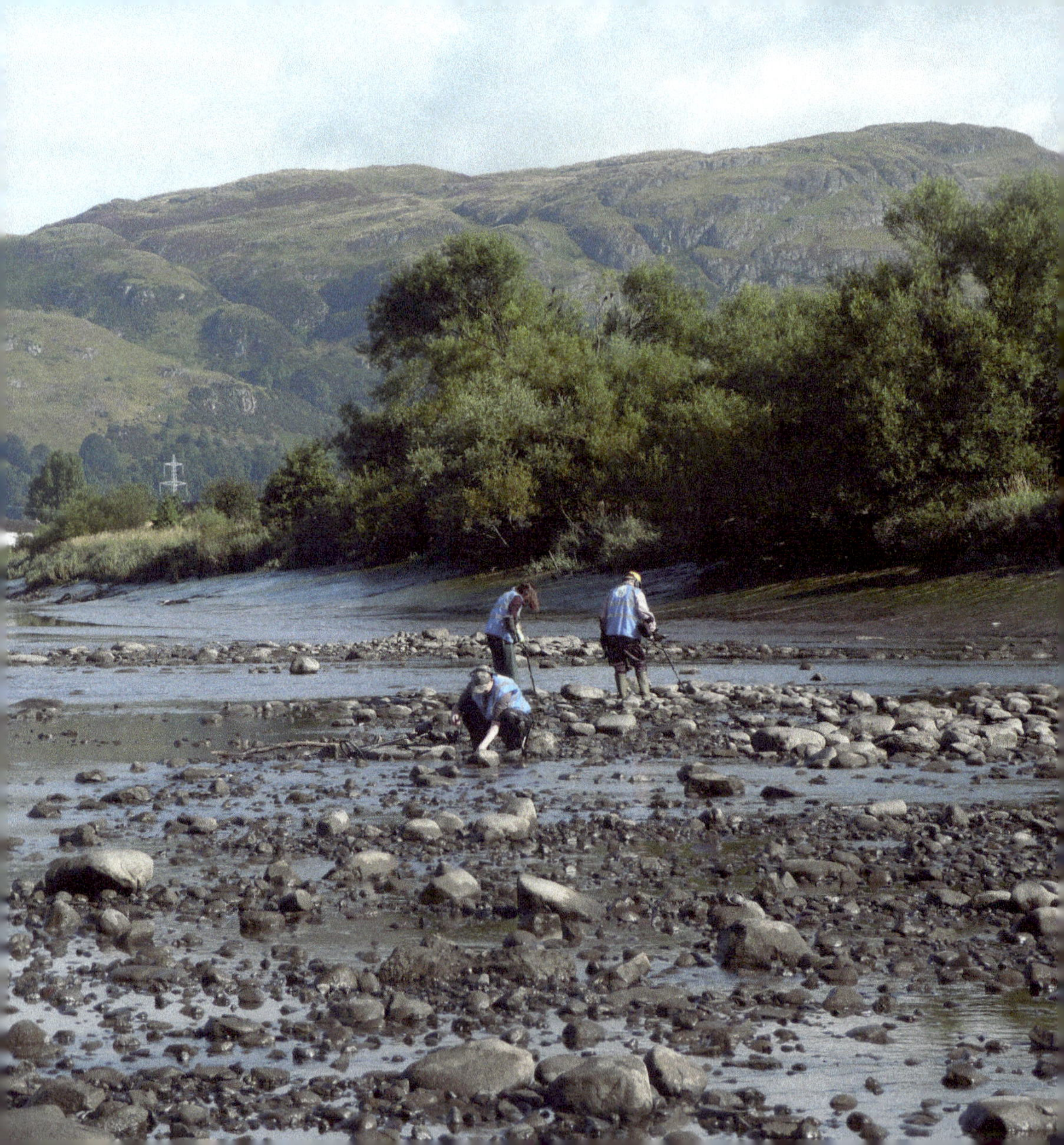

The Abbey Ford: Part 2

The Treacherous Earl of Atholl

As we've heard, the Battle of Bannockburn began with the siege of Stirling Castle, but where did the Bruce plan his campaign? We know he stayed at The Dominican Priory later on, and he had plotted in Cambuskenneth Abbey against Edward I during the 1304 siege. The Abbey was also where he would hold his first post-Bannockburn parliament, and where his coffin would rest before burial in Dunfermline. The Abbey was built in a meander of the Forth with water on three sides, and the tower has an excellent view of the castle to direct the siege. On balance we think this is where he plotted his deadly game of chess, and thus the only place on the battlefield we can link directly to Bruce.

Certainly, the Abbey was where Bruce's baggage train was guarded by Sir William of Airth, which was subject to a midnight raid at the conclusion of Day 1 of the battle by the renegade Scot John Strathbogie, Earl of Atholl, who had fallen out with the Bruce's family. As Barbour's *The Brus* put it:

That he apon Saynct Jhonys nicht,
Quen bath the kingis war boun to fight,
In Cammyskynnell the kingis vittaill,
He tuk and sadly gert assaile
Schyr Wilyam off Herth and him slew
And with him men ma then ynew.

We think Atholl and his men crossed the Abbey Ford in the dark—a daring and dangerous journey—but he had taken the wrong King's shilling and was no hero. After the battle, his lands and title were forfeited. He ended up working for the English as Constable of Northumbria, responsible for fending off the raids of his countrymen. His son would become a leading backer of Edward III during the second War of Independence, in a failed—if brutal—attempt to regain his titles and land. This too failed.

Again we suggest Cambuskenneth Abbey (NS 80840 93937) rather than the ford.

Balquidderock Wood
Where Exactly was the Battle of Bannockburn Fought?

Balquidderock Wood lies at the heart of Scotland's greatest military mystery: where was Day 2 of the Battle of Bannockburn fought? As you will remember, Day 1 was just a bloody nose for the English. Day 2, however, was where Bruce's legend was born and Scotland's freedom secured. But where did the first clash of weapons take place? The Scots were on the high ground to the south of the wood while the English where on the low boggy ground between the Pelstream and the Bannockburn, where the fighting ended up. The two locations are called respectively the Dryfield and the Wetfield. The written accounts suggest the Dryfield, but this would imply that the Scots waited for the English to march up the wood's slope before fighting, which raises the potential that the Scots would be surrounded. Today the location is open ground and playing fields, but its name is Broomridge which perhaps means the slopes were covered with dense thorny vegetation. The alternative Wetfield theory is that the Scots marched down the wood's slope to meet the English and prevent them deploying, in effect pushing the English cork back into the bottle of the Pelstream and Bannockburn which form the sharp tip of a V to the north.

We have debated this over the years; the Dryfield is required for the heavy horse but the water is in the Wetfield… but does it really matter? It was either an astonishing victory or an absolutely astonishing one! The key is that the fighting concluded in a rout and all order broke down; the Hammer of the Scots' son was himself hammered. The key extra factor was the arrival of the Sma' Folk (camp followers who had not been trained to fight) from the west, as they gave the appearance of fresh Scottish troops arriving to catch the English in the deadly jaws of a pincer. The real mystery is: did Bruce plan for their arrival, or was he just lucky?[6]

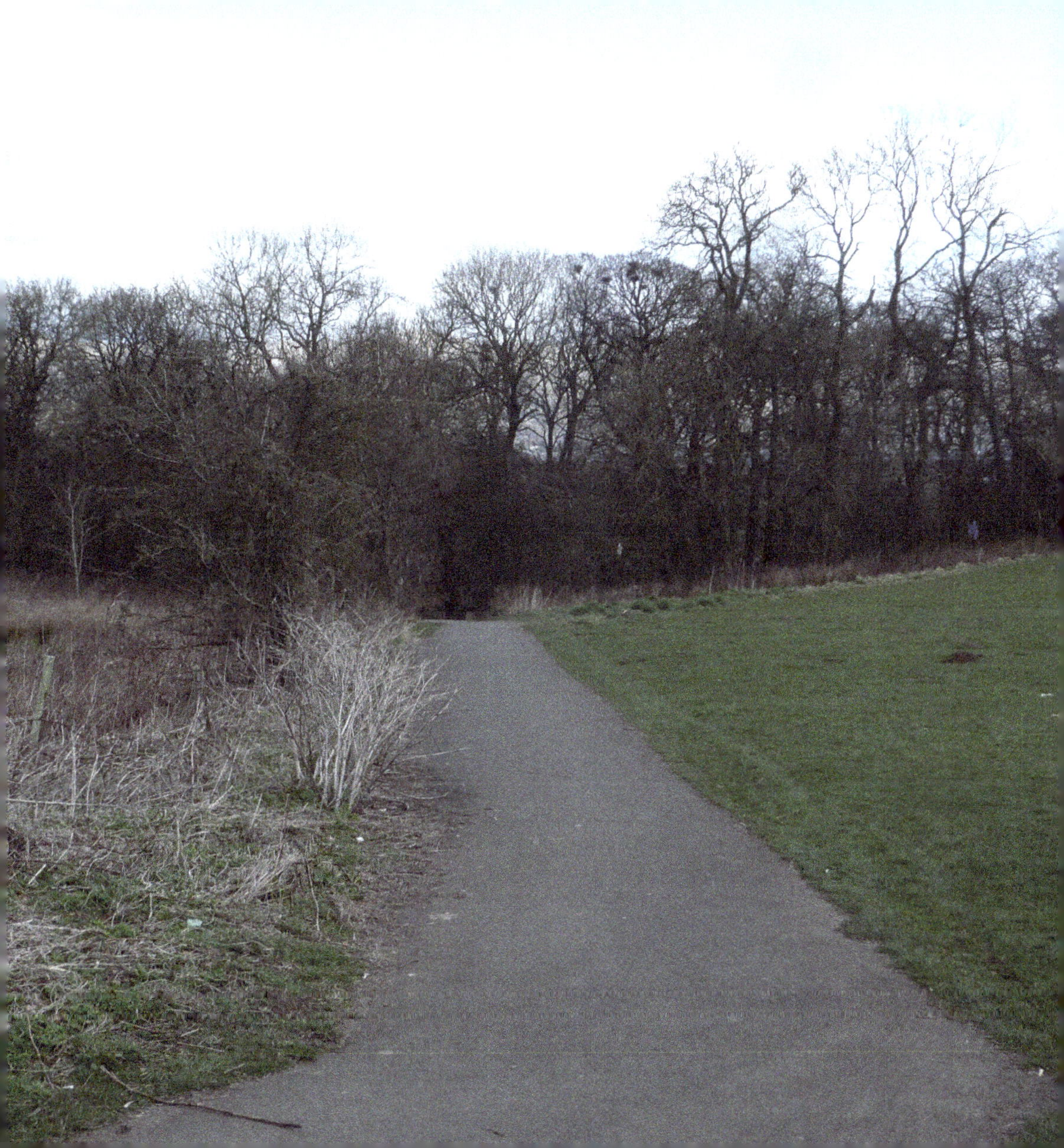

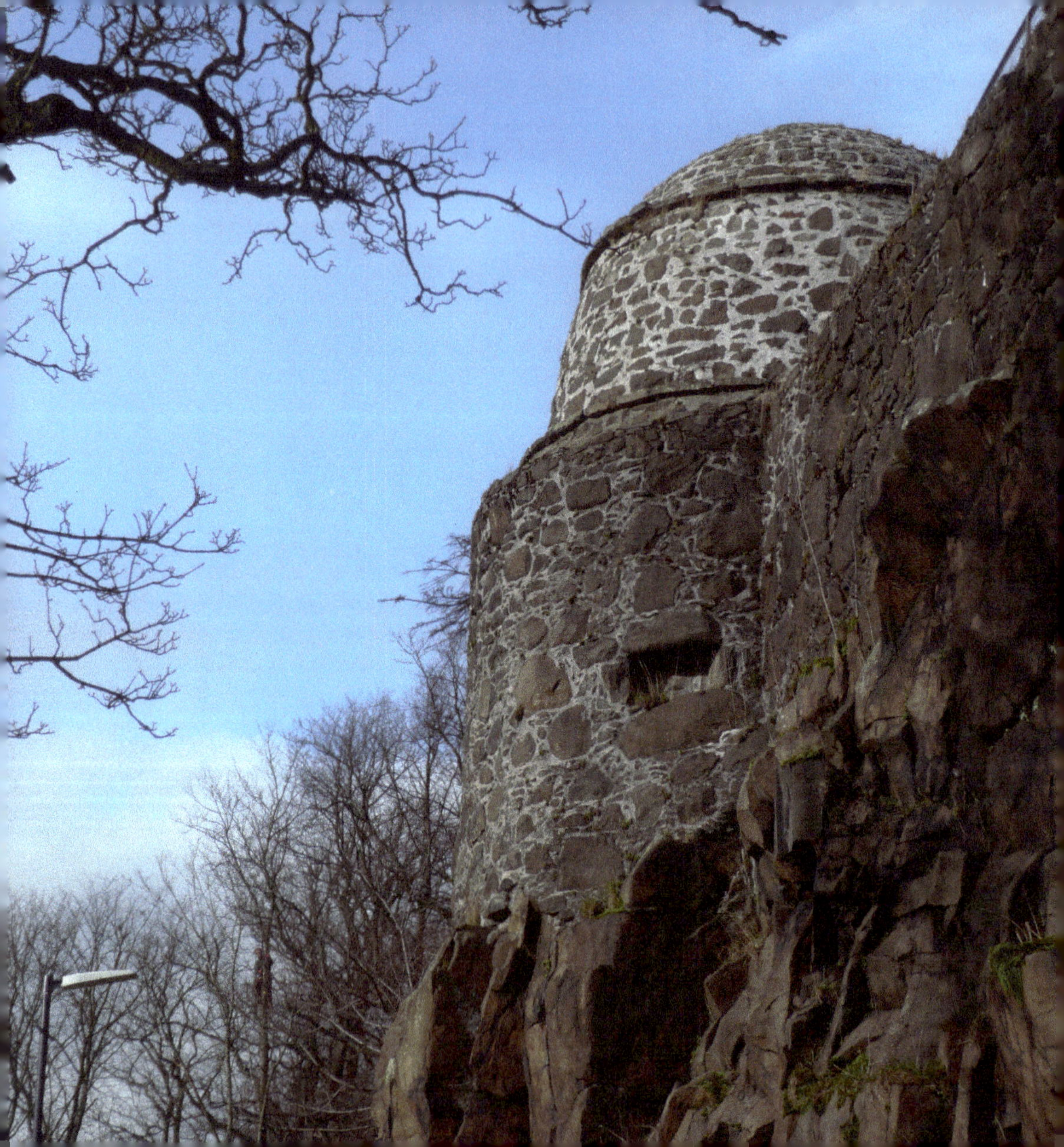

Guarding the Rock
Stirling's City Wall: The Best Preserved in Scotland

Famously, the price of peace is eternal vigilance. The picture here is one of the three best preserved watch towers on Stirling's City Wall, built in 1547 to deter the late Henry VIII's regent seizing Scotland. At the time, England was Protestant and Scotland Catholic and backed by France. The wall was only ever built on the south side of Stirling—no one expected to be attacked from the boggy ground to the north, which also had a massive 10m wide and 2m deep drainage ditch. Stirling's walls were never really tested, as Henry's troops never ventured that far.

In the 17th century, Cromwell's General in Scotland, Monck, captured the town without firing a shot and the castle surrendered after three days following a mutiny. Things were different on 5th January 1746 against Bonnie Prince Charlie's Highlanders. The walls and gates were secured against 8,000-9,000 Jacobites who had started to dig offensive positions. But the bog to the north had been drained, and the way in from the north was relatively open. To hasten a decision, the Jacobites fired 27 cannon shots into the town, and the townsfolk surrendered on the 8th. The walls were never used again, and are now a sleepy tourist attraction… thank goodness!

There were originally eight towers, and fragments of five survive. The best three are at Allan's Primary School playground (NS 24.3 79437 93421), the Youth Hostel on St John's Street (NS 24.2 79244 93568), and the third lies within the Thistles Shopping Centre and has been turned into a visitor centre (NS 24.4 79728 93276).

There is an awful lot of the wall to see, so we recommend the hard approach… park at the Stirling Smith Museum and Art Gallery (NS 24.1 79120 93494) and walk up the zig-zag path. Now imagine trying to do it running and under fire!

Mar's Wark

The Fatal Shooting of Scotland's Head of State

The deposition of Mary Queen of Scots and her replacement on the throne with her infant son James VI resulted in a very brief, if violent, Civil War. The Regent for the infant James VI was his grandfather, Matthew, 4th Earl of Lennox. On the 4th of September 1571 outside Mar's Wark there was a violent struggle with Mary's supporters, and Matthew was shot and died of his wounds within hours. While early reports suggested he was killed by his own men, the blame was eventually placed—rightly or wrongly—on Mary's shoulders. Of course, this meant James' mother could be accused of the death of both his father and grandfather: not a recipe for a happy childhood. James' hatred for his mum was so well known that she is absent from a scene in Shakespeare's *Macbeth* which shows the hero's descendants (including James himself).

The architect of Mar's Wark, which had been newly constructed using stones looted from Cambuskenneth Abbey, had obviously expected some kind of trouble because there are a series of small gun loops at each of the doorways. Just what you need to get rid of any cold callers! As an aside, while we don't know where the fatal gun was made, just up the road in Doune the village would eventually have an international reputation for gunsmiths. It is even said that the first shot of the American Revolution was from a Doune pistol.[7] The industry started with Thomas Caddell, who began making pistols in 1646. They were sold in pairs and were both deadly and attractive, and there was a weekly sale at the Market Cross which stands to this day.

Mar's Wark (25.1 NS 79226 93745) is easy to find. Parking is trickier though, but there are always spaces on Lower Bridge Street (25.2 NS 79420 94375).

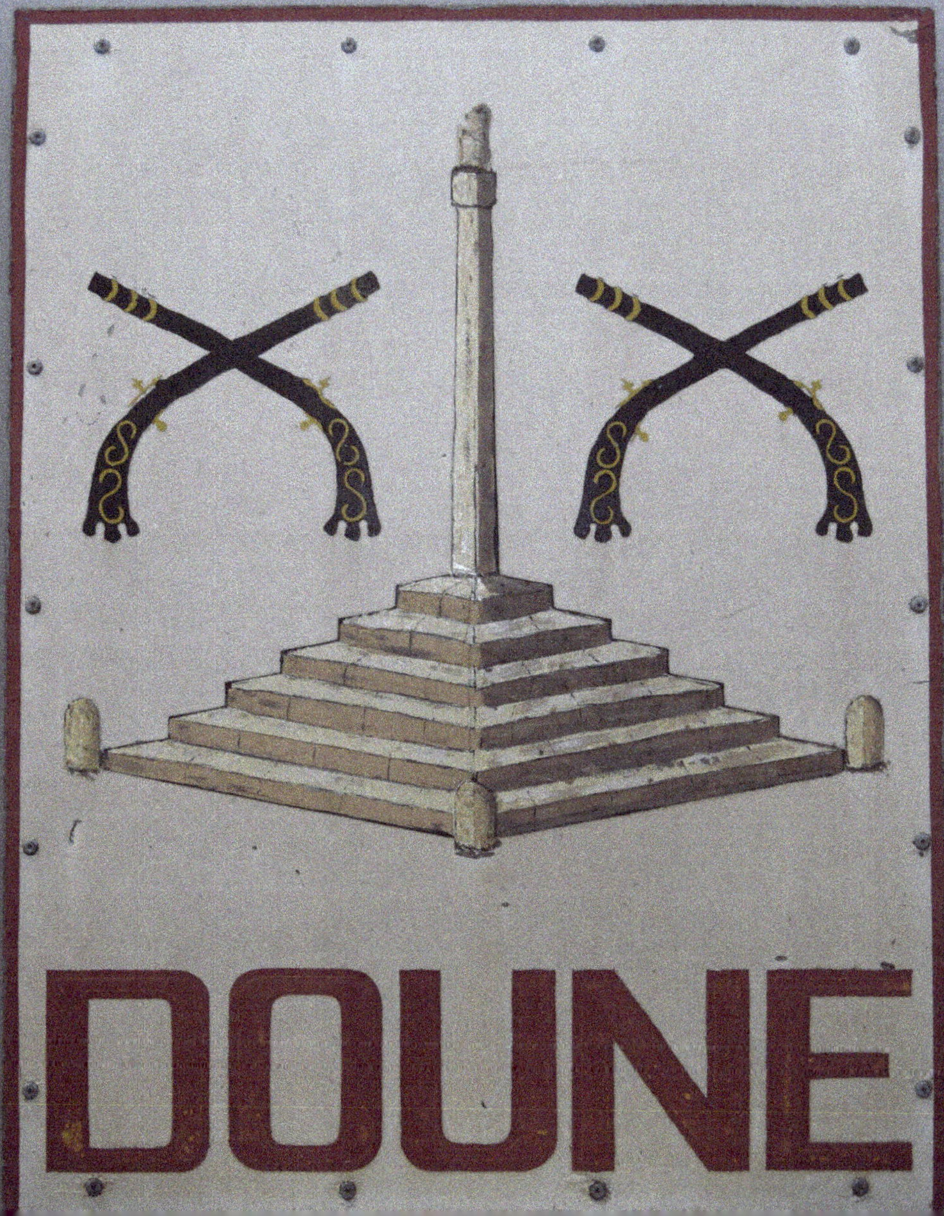
DOUNE

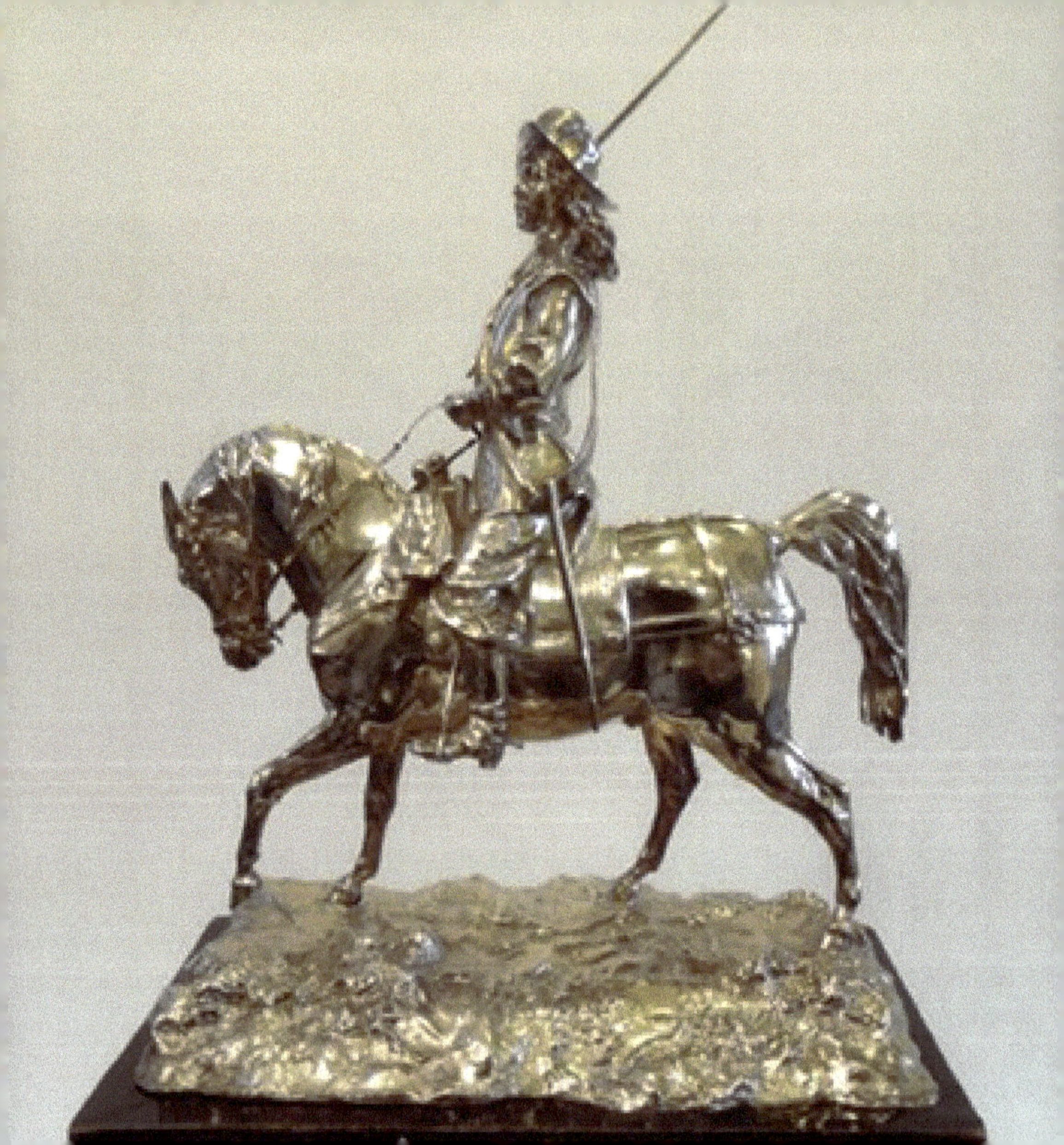

The Battle of Kilsyth

The Bloody End of Montrose

The 17th century was a particularly violent period for Scotland, with the Stuarts and their conflict with parliament scorching all of the British Isles. James Graham, 5th Earl of Montrose, was both a military genius and a pragmatist. Charles I—in a trend started by his dad James VI, and carried on by his son Charles II—wanted to exercise more control over the church. This led to the National Covenant of 1638, which guaranteed religious freedom for Presbyterians in Scotland. Montrose first fought for religious freedom against the King, but then fought on his side as he didn't want a theocracy.

Montrose led royalist forces to several victories in the Civil War during 1644–45, including Tippermore, Inverlochy and Alford. The Marquis of Argyll's Regiment, fore-runner of the Argyll and Sutherland Highlanders, was part of the losing government force. Montrose's most stunning victory was at Kilsyth in August 1645. His army bypassed the Covenanter-held Stirling, crossing the Forth at the Ford of Frew. These Royalists marched south overnight and arrived on the edge of the Campsies east of Kilsyth on 15th August. Montrose was pursued by a larger force led by General William Baillie which had burnt the grand houses of Menstrie and Airthrey who had supported the King. The two armies met at Banton and the battle was a stunning success for Montrose. However, eventually his luck ran out; he was subsequently captured and sentenced to death. His body was butchered, and Stirling got a leg which was pinned to the Barras Yett!

Following Charles II's restoration, Montrose was reassembled and buried with full honours in St Giles Cathedral in Edinburgh. Famously, ahead of D-Day, General Montgomery quoted one of Montrose's poems to motivate his troops:

'He either fears his Fate too much,
 Or his Deserts are small,
 That puts it not unto the Touch,
 To win or lose it all...'

Stirling's medieval gate—the Barras Yett—was demolished in the 18th century, but the location is marked by a plaque (NS 79665 93235).

The Church of the Holy Rude

The Cromwellian Siege of 1651

Following Cromwell's decision to execute Charles I, the Scots decided to support Charles II's bid for the English throne... d'oh! This resulted in the invasion, conquest and occupation of Scotland. As we have heard, Stirling's city walls were not tested and the castle only lasted three days. Lieutenant General Monck forced troops from the Church of the Holy Rude and then began to pound the castle. Impact damage is visible on the tower of the church itself, and the Chapel Royal inside the castle features damage from a mortar that landed in the central quad. There must have been some fighting within the cemetery, as the famous Service stone features musket ball impacts on both sides and the third window of the western face of the church's tower shows impacts aimed at a sniper operating out of the tiny window. While most of these missed the window, only one would've needed to get through as the possible ricochet would have shredded the sniper. There must've been other unrecorded skirmishes; for example, the tower at Cambuskenneth Abbey—used by the Bruces to monitor the Castle during the siege—was also used by a sniper, and their position was peppered by dozens of musket ball impacts too.

With Cromwell's death, the regime collapsed and Charles II was restored to the throne. But he had scores to settle. He thought that the Church of Scotland had demanded too much from him to support his claim to Britain's glittering throne, and he would impose his own controls on Protestant Christian worship in Scotland. This would begin with the beheading of the minister of the Church of the Holy Rude, James Guthrie—a man who Cromwell tolerated—and so started The Killing Times. Guthrie and the Solway Martyrs (executed for opposing Bishops!), along with James Renwick (the last Minister to be executed by the state), all have statues in the Old Town Cemetery, which also features an impressive pyramid to all martyrs for Presbyterian religious freedom.

If you've been to Mar's Wark, the church is just to the south (NS 79213 93713), and the tower is best viewed from the cemetery.

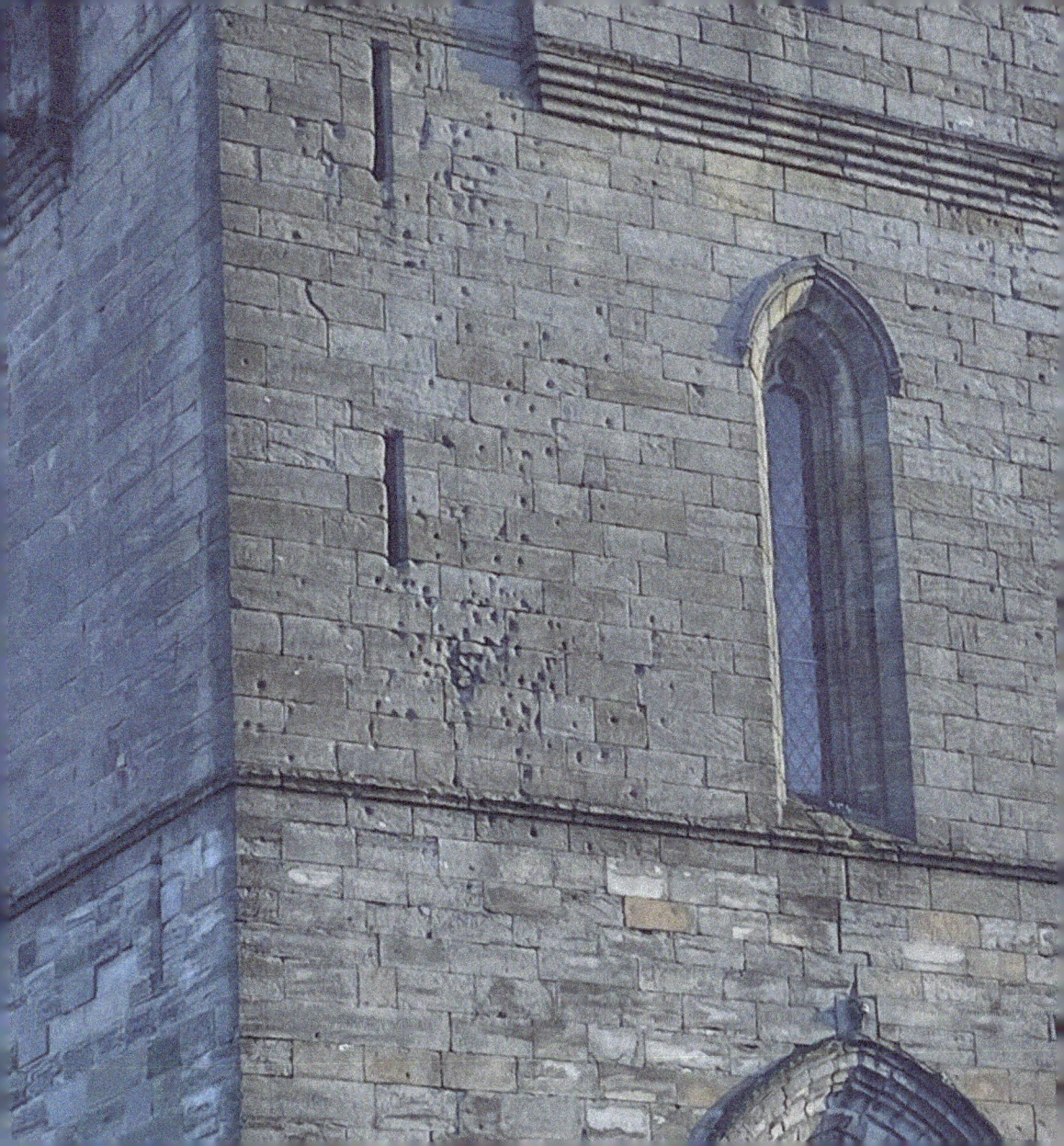

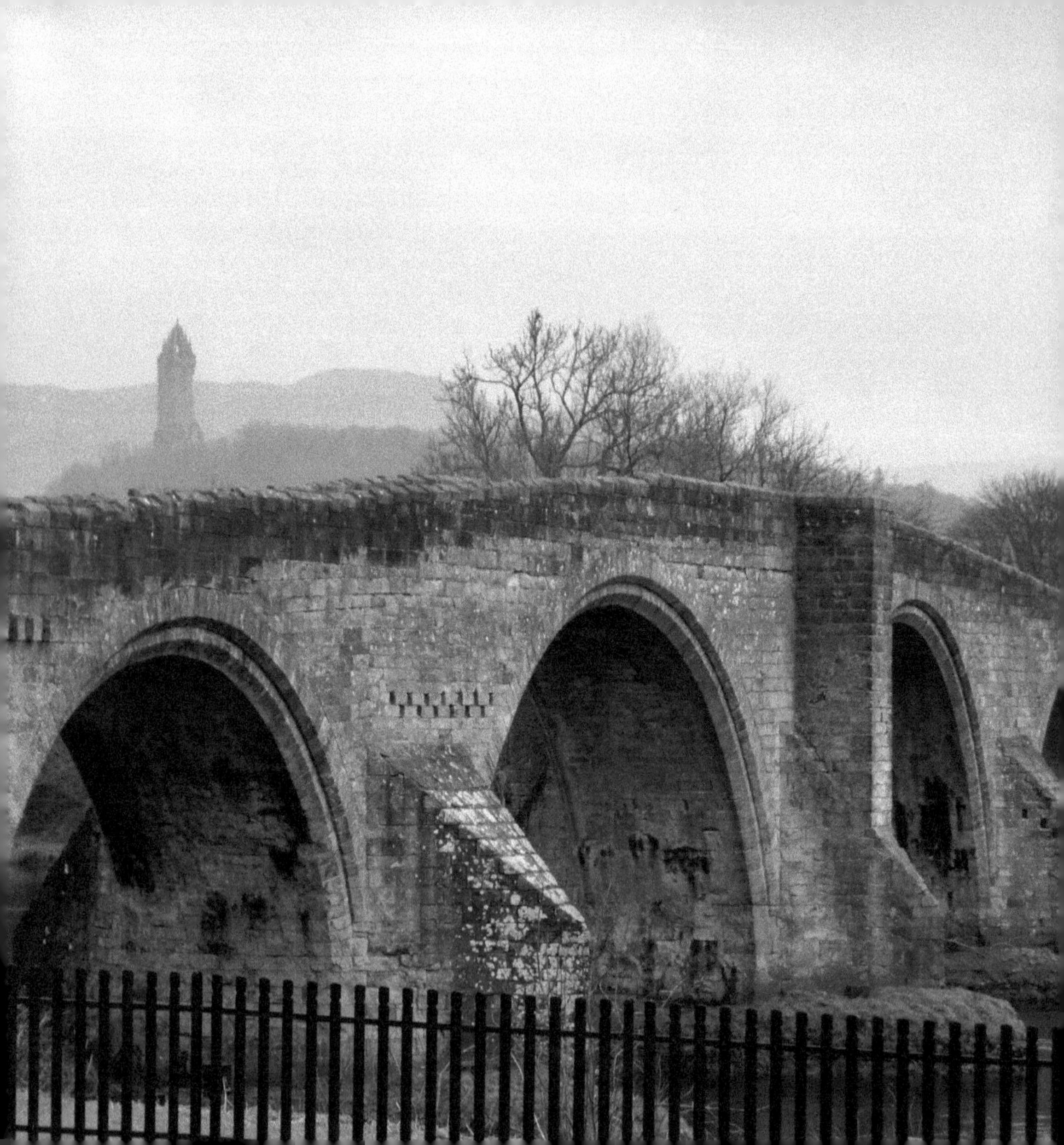

Stirling Bridge: Part 4

The Highland Host and its Bloody Wake

As we've heard, Charles II wished to control how Scots worshipped Christ. This was not a Protestant/Catholic division—which had scarred Europe for centuries, and still wounds Northern Ireland—but rather differing interpretations of Protestantism. To be simplistic, the more radical minority elements of the Church of Scotland would brook no interference in the relationship between a congregation and their minister, while Charles and later his brother James VII wanted to set a common prayer book and introduce Bishops who would be appointed by the state. This was contrary to what Charles II and his dad Charles I had agreed to when they signed The National Covenant.

The more radical elements took to worshipping outdoors (Field Conventicles), and the people who supported this were called Covenanters. The state was so outraged by this that eventually soldiers were ordered to break up the Field Conventicles. A force was drawn from the Highlands and, on 24th January 1678, 6,000–7,000 Highlanders were joined by 3,000 regular troops at Stirling Bridge.

This host monitored Ayrshire, Renfrewshire, and Lanarkshire with a resulting litany of brutality, theft and murder. In Kilmarnock, men quartered with William Dickie apparently stabbed his pregnant wife—who died as a result—and then they beat him up. Others, including Church of Scotland Ministers, died of their beatings, and the Host departed with a considerable volume of loot. This heavy-handed state-sponsored terrorism so inflamed opinion that it clearly contributed to the Battle of Bothwell Brig the year after, to which Kippen Minister James Ure led 200 armed men. While the Covenanters lost this battle, they would eventually be triumphant after the 'Glorious Revolution' of 1689 when James VII was deposed. While this was largely bloodless in England, there was much bloodshed and death in the other two Kingdoms of Ireland and Scotland.

Back and Forth
Guarding the Forth's Crossings Against the Jacobites

We have heard of the strategic significance of Drip Ford over the centuries and how it was watched by Edward I's spies. From the Glorious Revolution to the '45, the state was constantly worried about securing all of the crossings over the Forth to prevent Jacobite armies swarming south. In May 1689, the new Government ordered 300 men to guard the passes of the Forth centred on Drip, and the same locations had soldiers stationed in 1715 and 1745. In 1715 the Jacobites anticipated that the Government had '*spoilt*' the fords by '*digging and putting great beams in them with iron spikes*'; apparently Rob Roy knew of some other options, but no one trusted him! To make matters worse, the castle's cannons could fire upon Drip.

This was, of course, why Bonnie Prince Charlie and his Jacobite army crossed in secret at the Ford of Frew on 13th September 1745 on the march to Derby. Despite its modern reputation (all of which is based on the novels of Walter Scott and John Buchan), this was a small ford used by no-one but locals, and which added several miles to the trip. It worked though, and while the Government's troops led by Sir John Cope was in Inverness the Prince passed Stirling Castle.

After Derby the Jacobites were planning to capture Stirling Castle as winter quarters, but General Blakeney prepared a trap for them by cutting the inner arch of Stirling Bridge. The Jacobites would be between the anvil of Stirling Castle and Henry 'Hangman' Hawley's hammer: a Government army heading north. While the Jacobites won this battle (the second Battle of Falkirk), the siege did not end well and they fled north ahead of the more competent Cumberland. They apparently used the Ford of Frew again, but the conditions were worse and they had to abandon at least one cannon.

We have not given a location to this ford, which is very hard to access and—according to local tradition—is a secret Jacobite one!

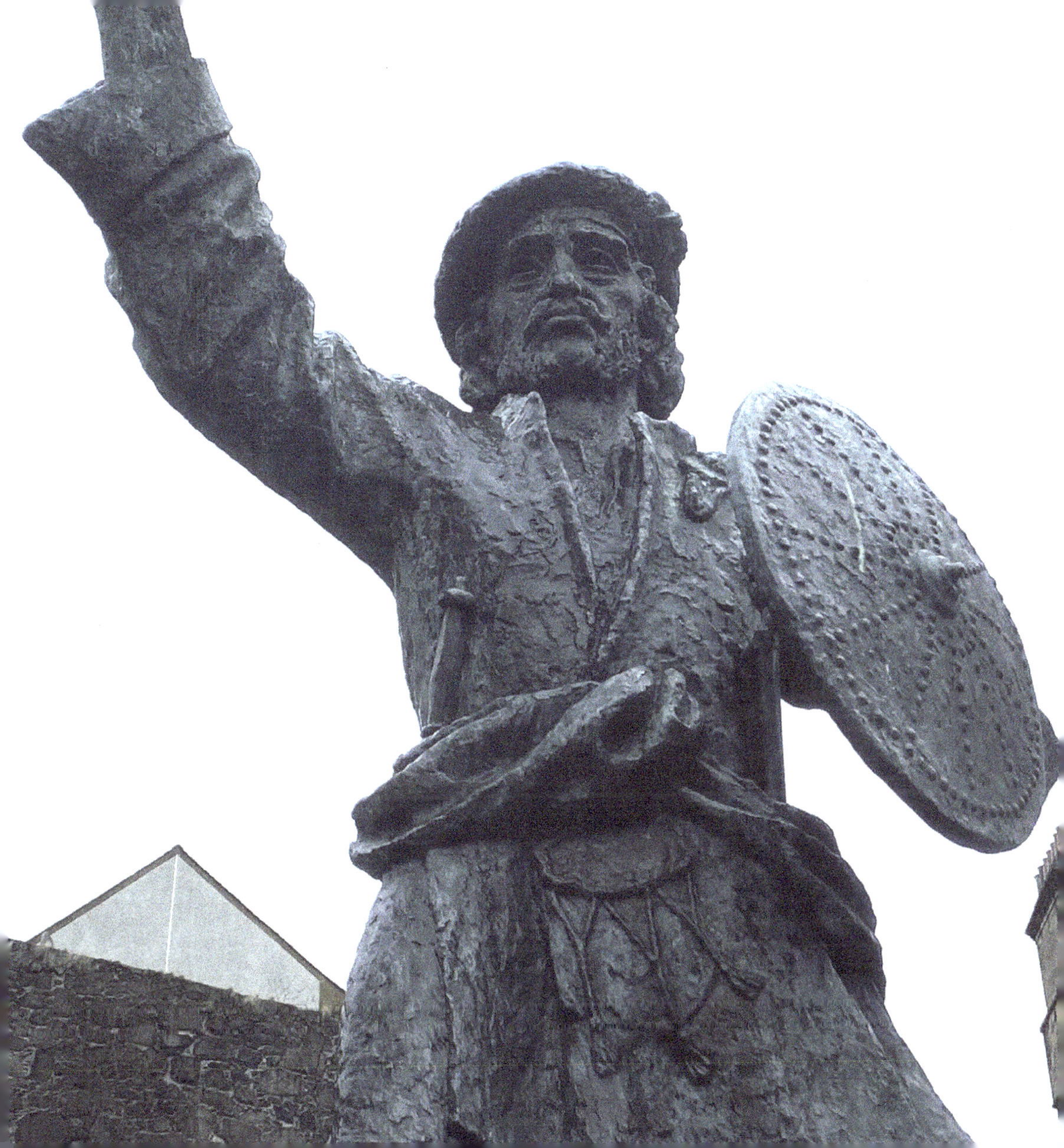

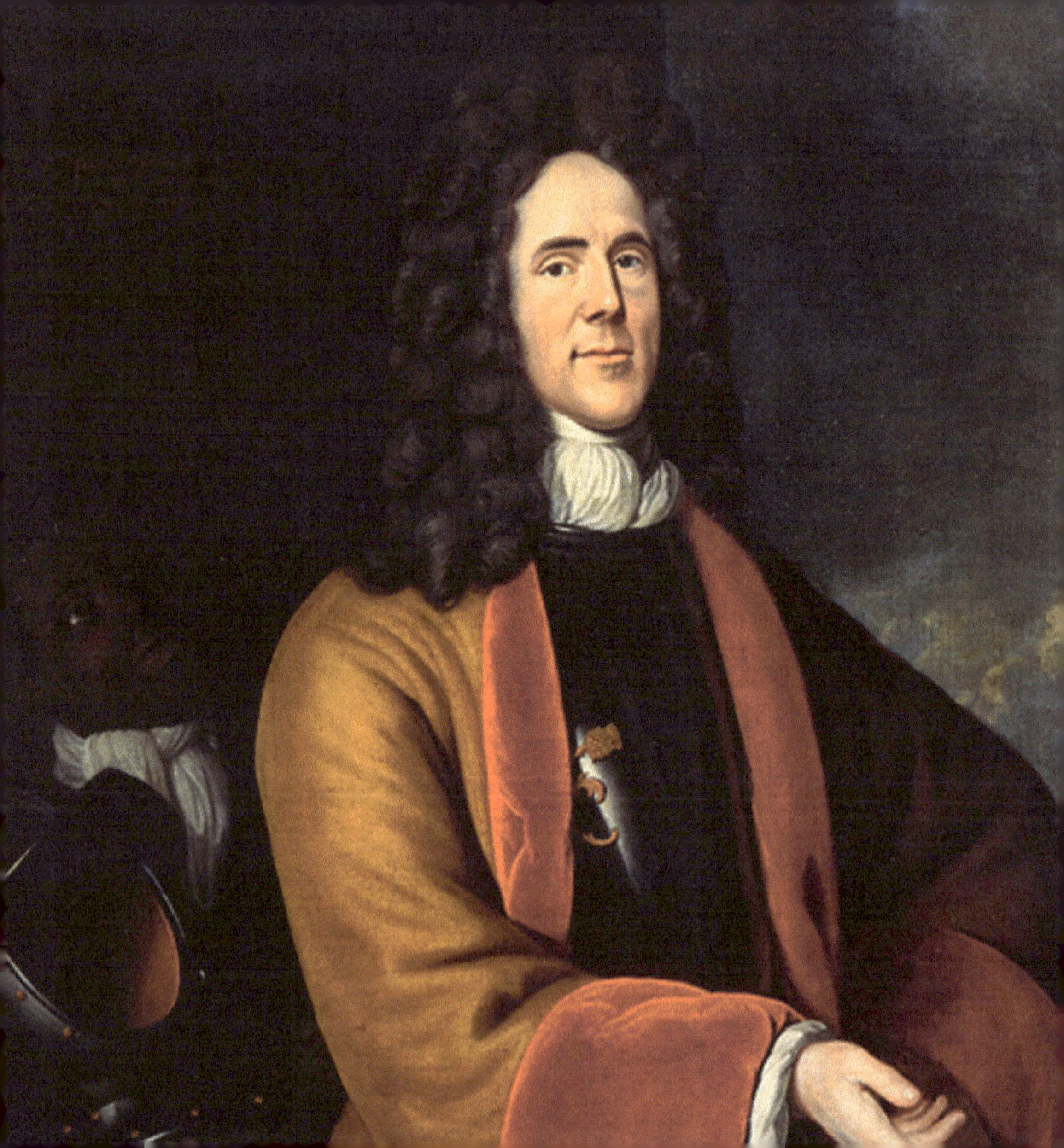

The Battle of Sheriffmuir

Blackadder's Cunning Plan

The Rising of 1715 began when the Earl of Mar (the same family as Mar's Wark) proclaimed James III and VIII the rightful King, rather than the Hanoverian George I. At the time, the battle was named Dunblane, rather than Sheriffmuir,[8] since the main Redcoat strategy was stopping the Jacobites crossing the Forth by blocking their passage on the main road through Dunblane. It seems clear that the British Army deployed with its left-wing cavalry next to the River Allan (probably on Holme Hill), with the infantry in line along the road which passes the Hydro and the right wing cavalry, including the Scots Greys, stretching towards Dykedale farm.

When they realised that the road was blocked by the government forces, the Jacobites swung to the east onto the higher ground, still heading for the Forth down the Allan Water. The Redcoats moved up the hill to meet them, and the battle began. The British Army's right defeated the Jacobites, while the Highlanders routed the Redcoats' left.

There's some say that we wan,
And some say that they wan,
And some say that nane wan at a', man;
But one thing I'm sure,
That at Sherra-muir,
A battle there was that I saw, man;
And we ran, and they ran,
And they ran, and we ran,
But Florence ran fastest of a', man.

However, even if they had won the day, Stirling Bridge and the various fords across the Forth were all guarded. Stirling Bridge with its two bridge gates was guarded by a militia from Glasgow and commanded by Colonel John Blackadder, whose father had been a staunch Presbyterian who had died as a result of being imprisoned on the Bass Rock at North Berwick. There was really no need for any cunning plan; the Jacobites were simply ground down. To escape, they burnt every village between Stirling and Perth, ensuring both a miserable Christmas for the locals and that very few came out for Bonnie Prince Charlie in the '45!

Back to the Church of the Holy Rude—inside, this time!

The '45
The Last Siege of Stirling Castle and the Destruction of St Ninians Church

In the wake of the '15, a network of roads was constructed by the Government to allow rapid troop movements to potential Jacobite hotspots—a great improvement on what had existed before:

Had you seen these roads before they were made
You would lift up your hands and bless General Wade

Many of these roads can be found locally, including the A811, but of course they allowed the Jacobites to move rapidly too! So when General Cope was marching to Inverness in hot pursuit of Bonnie Prince Charlie, the Young Pretender was marching cheerily past Stirling, having first crossed the Ford of Frew. Cope eventually caught them up at Prestonpans, but his forces collapsed against the Highland Charge: where muskets are fired as Highlanders charged, then dropped and swords drawn. Allegedly, the General stayed in bed until it was too late… not waking up in time!

Hey! Johnnie Cope are ye waukin' yet?
Or are your drums a-beating yet?
If ye were waukin' I wad wait,
Tae gang tae the coals in the morning.

After Black Friday and the retreat from Derby, the Jacobites planned for winter quarters at Stirling. The town surrendered after a short siege but the castle—in its last ever siege—held out all through January 1746, destroying each Jacobite artillery position: the first on our old friend Ladies Rock and the second on Gowan Hill to the castle's north (NS 79172 94117). Now, while the Prince's forces won the second Battle of Falkirk, there was confusion, they failed to maintain their advantage, and a smaller force returned to Stirling. The siege ended as Cumberland's troops marched north, entering Stirling at the start of February. In the commotion, the Jacobites managed to blow up their own gunpowder store at the St Ninians Kirk… ouch!

While St Ninians graveyard is closed to the public, the broken stumps of the mediaeval St Ninians Kirk are clearly visible (NS 79554 91687).

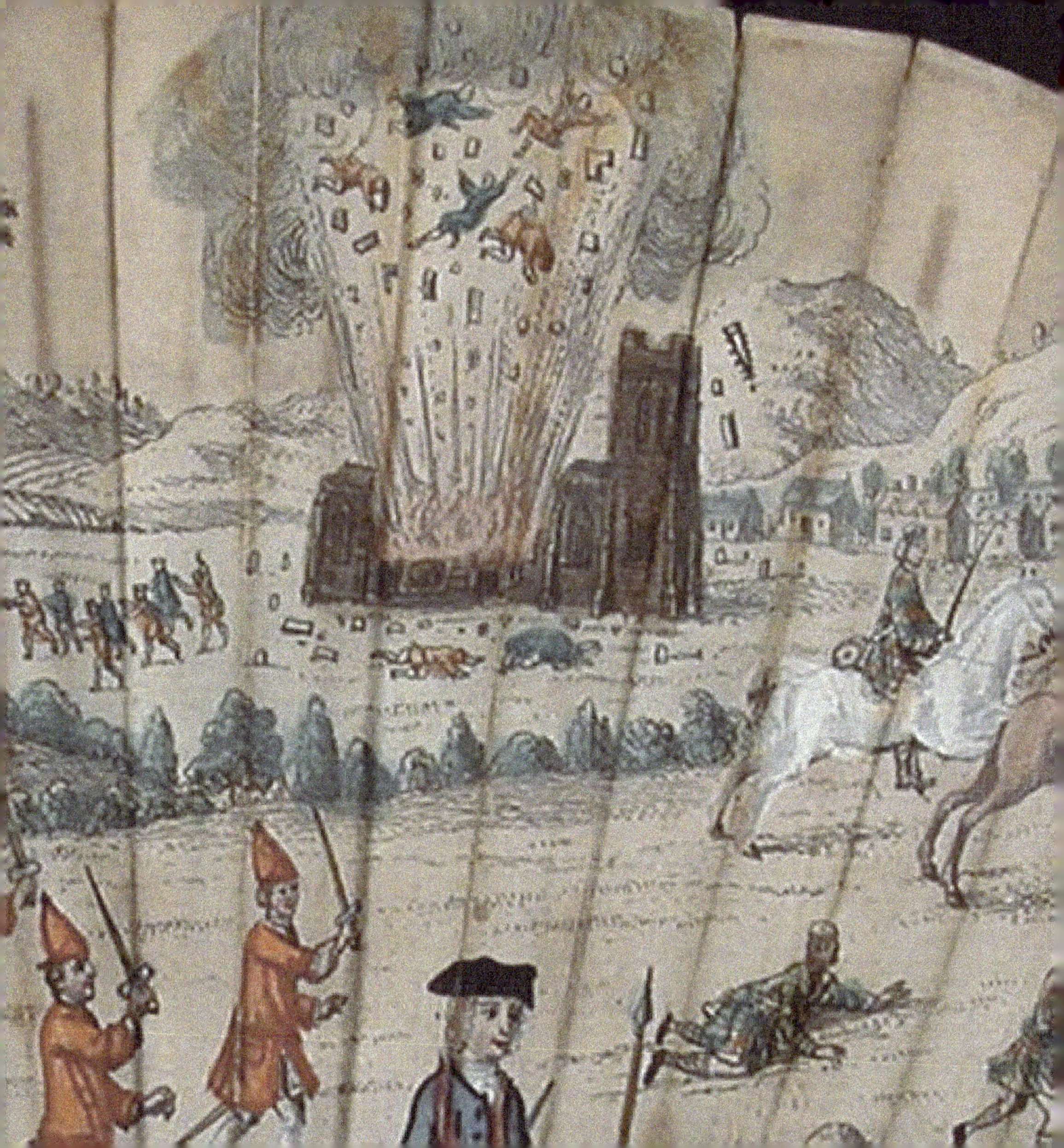

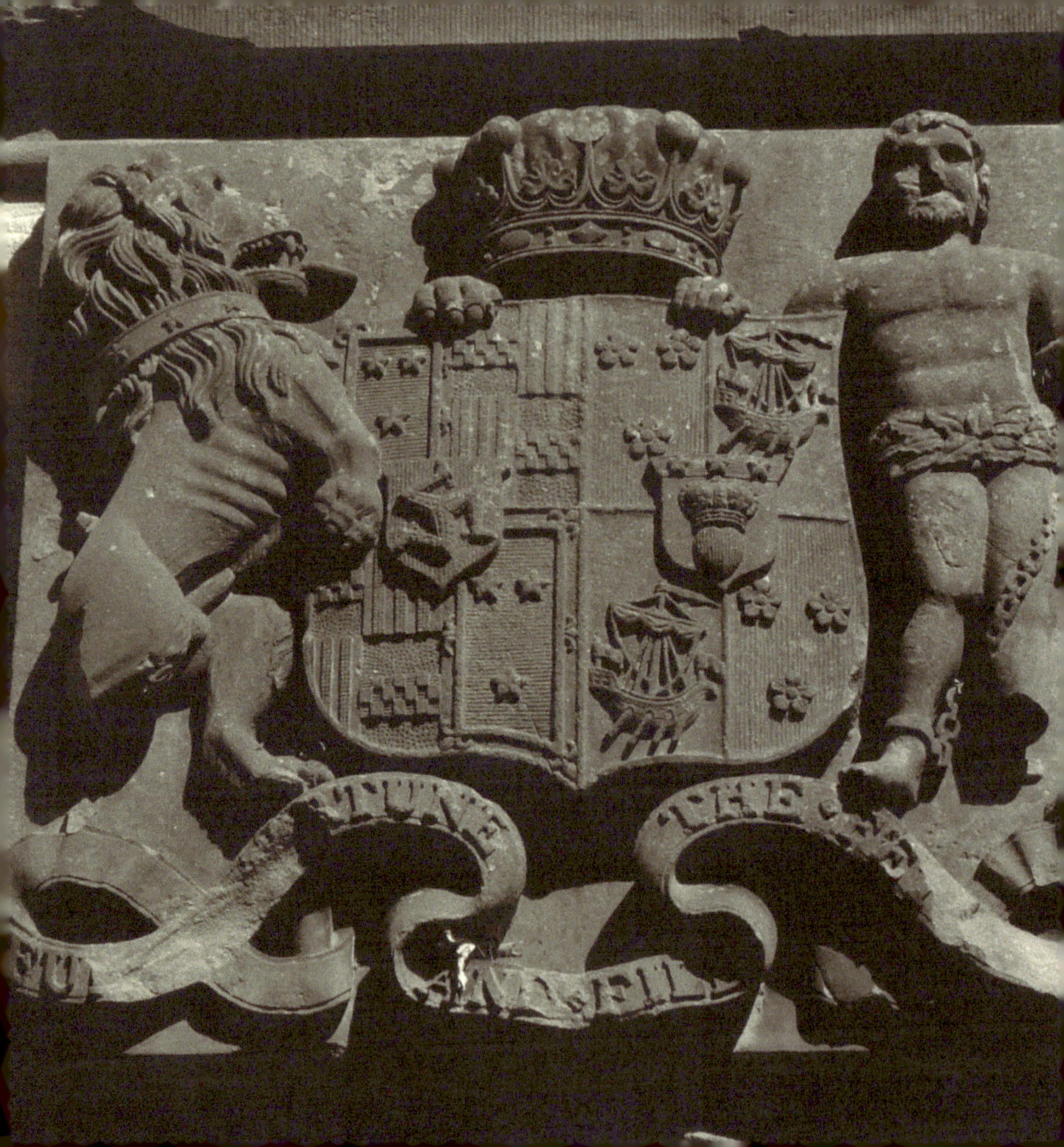
TUNE
THE

The 4th Earl of Dunmore
Scotland's First Slavery Abolitionist?

War makes for strange allies and desperate throws of the dice. John Murray, the Earl of Dunmore, was the last Colonial Governor of Virginia, but as a 15 year old he travelled with Bonnie Prince Charlie from the Ford of Frew to Culloden. After a royal pardon he became Governor of New York in 1770, and then Governor of Virginia where he was in charge of resistance to the Patriots. He issued the so-called Dunmore Proclamation of 1775 which promised freedom to any slave who joined his forces. It's estimated that between 800 and 2,000 slaves escaped to join what became known as Dunmore's Ethiopian Brigade. The Virginian Convention's response chillingly promised to execute any escaped slaves without *'the benefit of a Christian minister'*, i.e. their soul would be condemned too. While they saw some success, most died of a smallpox outbreak and only some 300 people escaped with Dunmore back to Britain. The tactic was tried again later on, and some 3,000 former slaves were relocated to Nova Scotia.

The Dunmores were very proud of this act and Dunmore House, Airth, shows a liberated slave on its coat of arms at the entrance. But very clearly this was a cynical act by a failing regime which had previously profited the taxes from business and farms that used slaves. Dunmore himself was a slave owner, and—in a telling line on his *'lost property'* following the American Revolution—made mention of between 100–150 people; surely his lack of precision was an indication of the value he placed on these exploited and truncated lives? Dunmore House's grounds features the famous Pineapple House built in 1761 by the Earl, but where did the money come from? Was it too a product of the slave economy?

The Dunmore Estate is a great day out with free if limited parking (NS 89003 88493), and don't miss the Pineapple!

Samuel Graham

His Brush with General George Washington

There is a clear roguish charm to the face opposite: a smile playing on the lips, and a twinkle to his remaining eye. This is Lieutenant General Samuel Graham, originally from Paisley, who became the Deputy Governor of Stirling Castle in 1800 and is buried in the Church of Holy Rude. He had fought for Britain across several continents, but this story concerns his service as a Captain in 76th Regiment of Foot (MacDonald's Highlanders) during the American Revolutionary War and the Asgill Affair.

Towards the end of the American Revolutionary War, tit-for-tat killings on both sides became commonplace. In May 1782, one Philip White (a British loyalist) was captured and offered a chance to run but was shot in the back after thirty yards. In turn, Loyalist irregular forces killed an American Captain, Joshua Huddy. In response to this, General Washington—in contravention of the articles of surrender following the siege of Yorktown—ordered a lottery of death. Thirteen British Captains (including Graham), all prisoners of war, were to be subject to the lottery, contrary to the terms of the Yorktown surrender. Captain Charles Asgill was selected but not executed due to protests by the French who were the Americans' allies. The French protests were led by the Queen Marie Antoinette (who would later be executed during the French Revolution), and she described it as enough to '*shock the heart of a savage*'.

The matter was ultimately decided by Congress, who narrowly voted to release Captain Asgill and send him back to Britain. It is clear that this damaged General Washington's reputation, and there is some evidence of an American smear campaign against Asgill to somehow justify Washington's actions... politics was ever a murky business! However, to return to our hero General Graham: his small role in the tale was well-known and a regular topic at the dinner table. After all, Graham may have been the one to draw the paper marked 'unfortunate', rather than Asgill.

Inside the Church of the Holy Rude again!

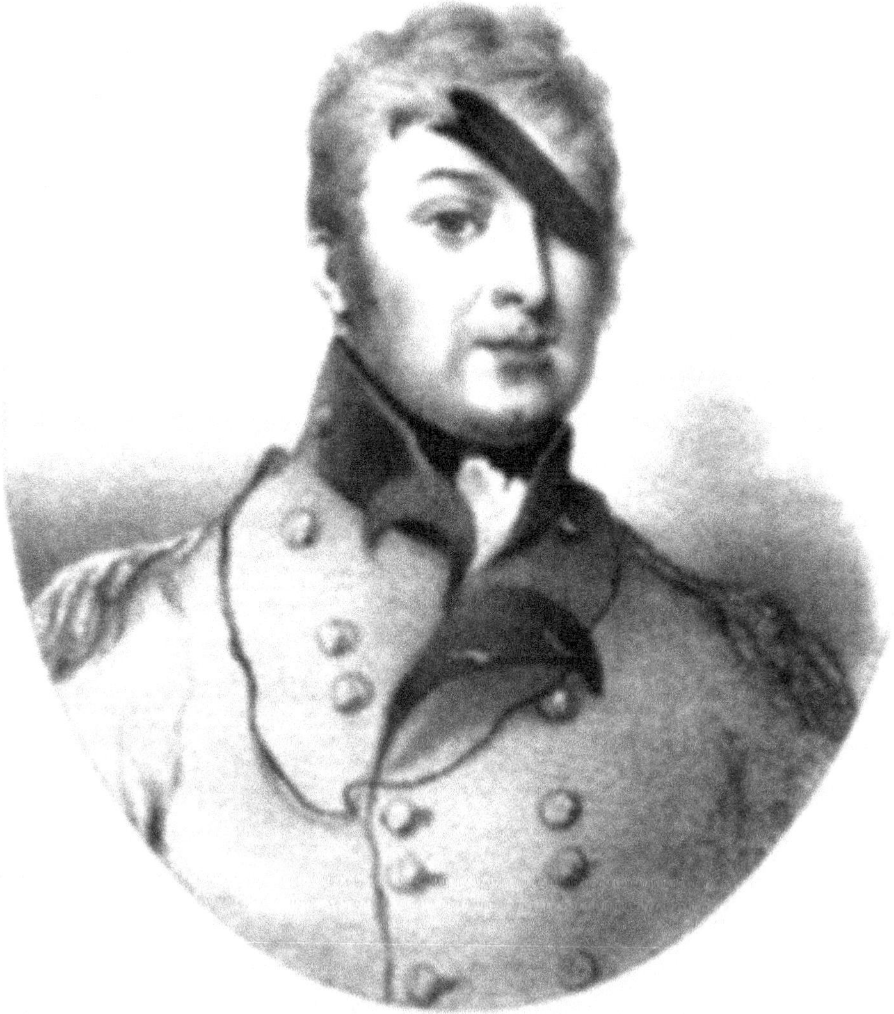

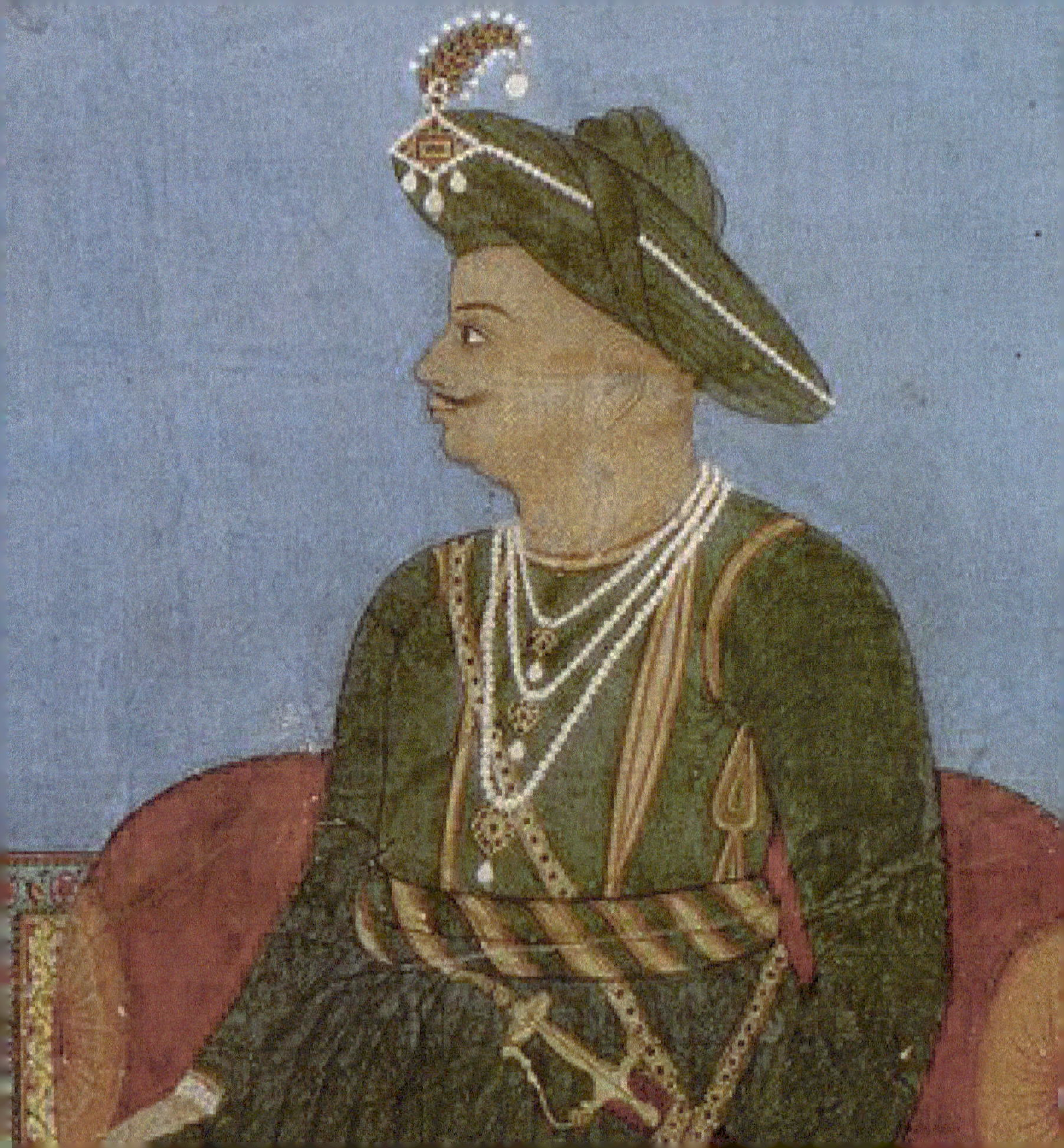

Marcus Marr
and the Tiger of Mysore

Lieutenant Marcus Marr died in 1799, aged 27. Marcus served in the 71st (Highland) Regiment of Foot and was an Ensign in 1789 at 17 after transferring from another force. His regiment fought in India in support of the East India Company in the 1790s. Another soldier's account of the trip to India in 1781 describes a yearlong passage round the Cape of Good Hope in which one fifth of the men died. Indeed, so terrible was the prospect that the first Scots regiment to be ordered to go rebelled! While kilts were initially taken, they were soon abandoned in the heat.

The main conflict of Marcus's career was in 1792 against Tipu Sultan (Sultan Fateh Ali Sahab Tipu), The Tiger of Mysore, at the siege of Seringaptam (Srirangapatna) in which Tipu was defeated. A force of 26,000 locally-recruited Indian soldiers of the East India Company, reinforced by 4,000 regular British troops and 20,000 Indians of the Nizam of Hyderabad, defeated the besieged army of Tipu Sultan, numbering 30,000. Marcus appears to have died shortly after returning to Stirling Castle, where the regiment was stationed, and his fellow officers paid for the stone.

Tipu and his father Haidar Ali (*Haidarāli*) were independent Muslim rulers of the Kingdom of Mysore. They had resisted the British invasions for 50 years. The wealth and exuberance of Mysore were astonishing, and thus clearly a target for the East India Company—as was the whole of India, which Sir Walter Scott described as a '*corn chest for Scotland*'! Tipu was obsessed with tigers, and even kept some as pets. However, Britain's invasion effectively collapsed local government and created chaos. Perhaps the most eloquent example of this was after the capture of Mysore, when the future Duke of Wellington had Tipu Sultan's tigers shot as there was no one to look after and feed them. Interestingly, part of the British force was led by Sir Thomas Abercromby, whose family gave their name to several locations in Bridge of Allan.

To the left of the modern entrance of the Church of the Holy Rude is Marcus Marr's modest memorial.

Airthrey
Empire and the Abercrombys

Airthrey Castle (now part of Stirling University) was rebuilt by the Haldane family with money made from the East India Company. In turn, it became the home of the Abercromby family who fought for Empire in the second half of the 18th century. Our story concerns three brothers: Ralph, Robert and James, all originally from Menstrie Castle which was burnt by the Covenanters. Between them, they fought across Europe, North America, Canada, India, the Caribbean and Egypt, and Robert founded Stirling's Regiment... the 75th Regiment of Foot. The American Revolutionary Wars split the brothers; Ralph supported the colonists and avoided fighting, but Robert and James fought for their King and James died at the Battle of Brooklyn.

Ralph fought Revolutionary France when they declared war on Britain. His first engagement was as a Brigade commander in the ill-fated 1809 expedition in the Netherlands, which was famously mocked in the children's rhyme:

Oh, the grand old Duke of York,
He had ten thousand men;
He marched them up to the top of the hill,
And he marched them down again.

However, Ralph also helped suppress the Irish rebellion of 1798 and the Grenada slave revolt of 1795. In 1801, Ralph was ordered to clear the French from Egypt and managed a successful landing at Aboukir. He was victorious at the Battle of Alexandria, but was fatally wounded and died on 28th March 1801.

In 1788, Robert travelled to India and successively became a general in the army, Governor of Bombay and Commander-in-Chief of the Bombay Army and then Commander-in-Chief, India. Although he had a reputation for honesty, these positions helped him accrue a fortune, and he returned home as a nabob to buy Airthrey and was instrumental in developing Bridge of Allan as a Victorian spa town, despite his deteriorating eyesight and eventual blindness.

Airthrey Castle (NS 81225 96712) is part of Stirling University, the grounds of which are open to the public: a great series of walks!

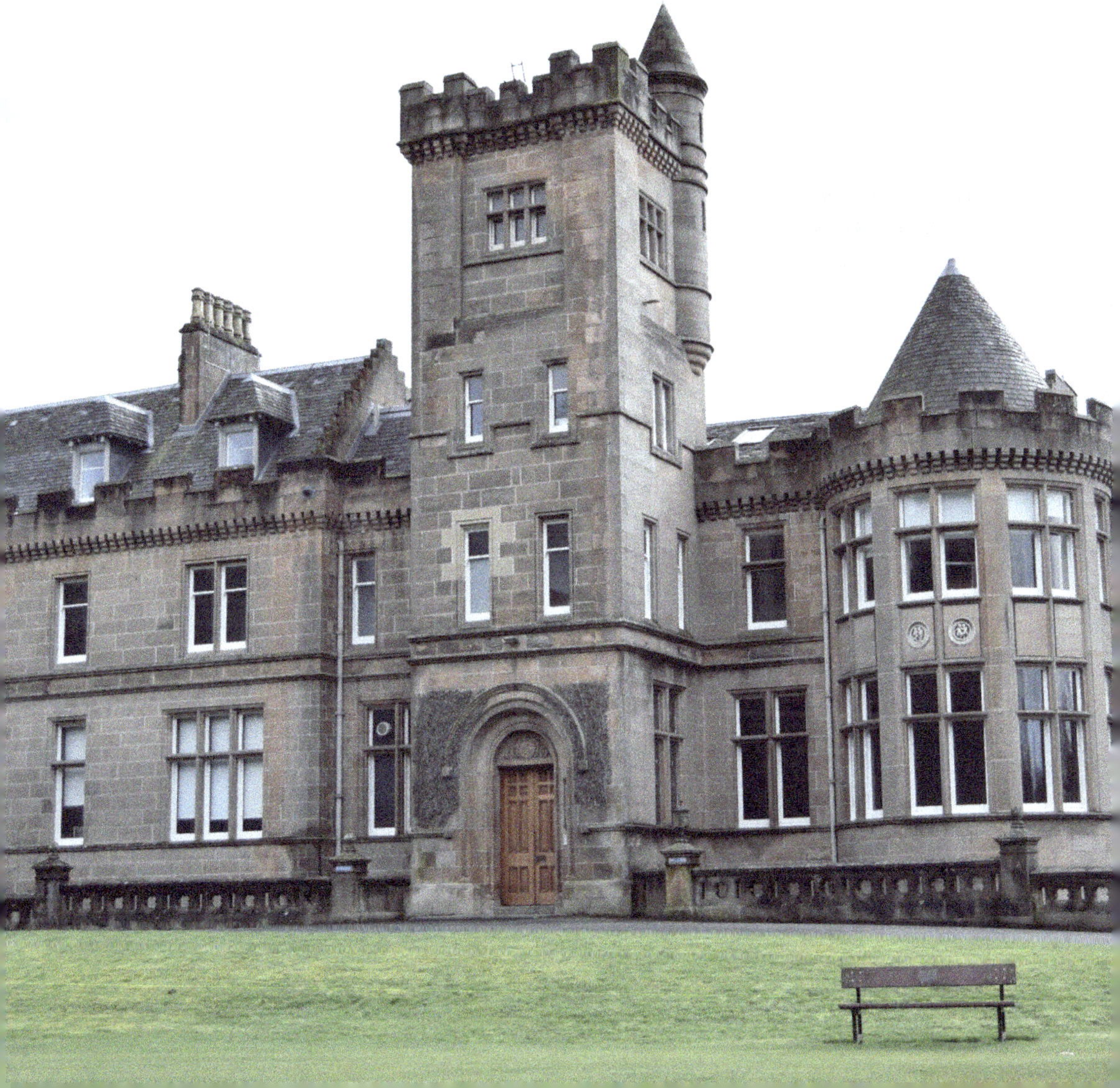

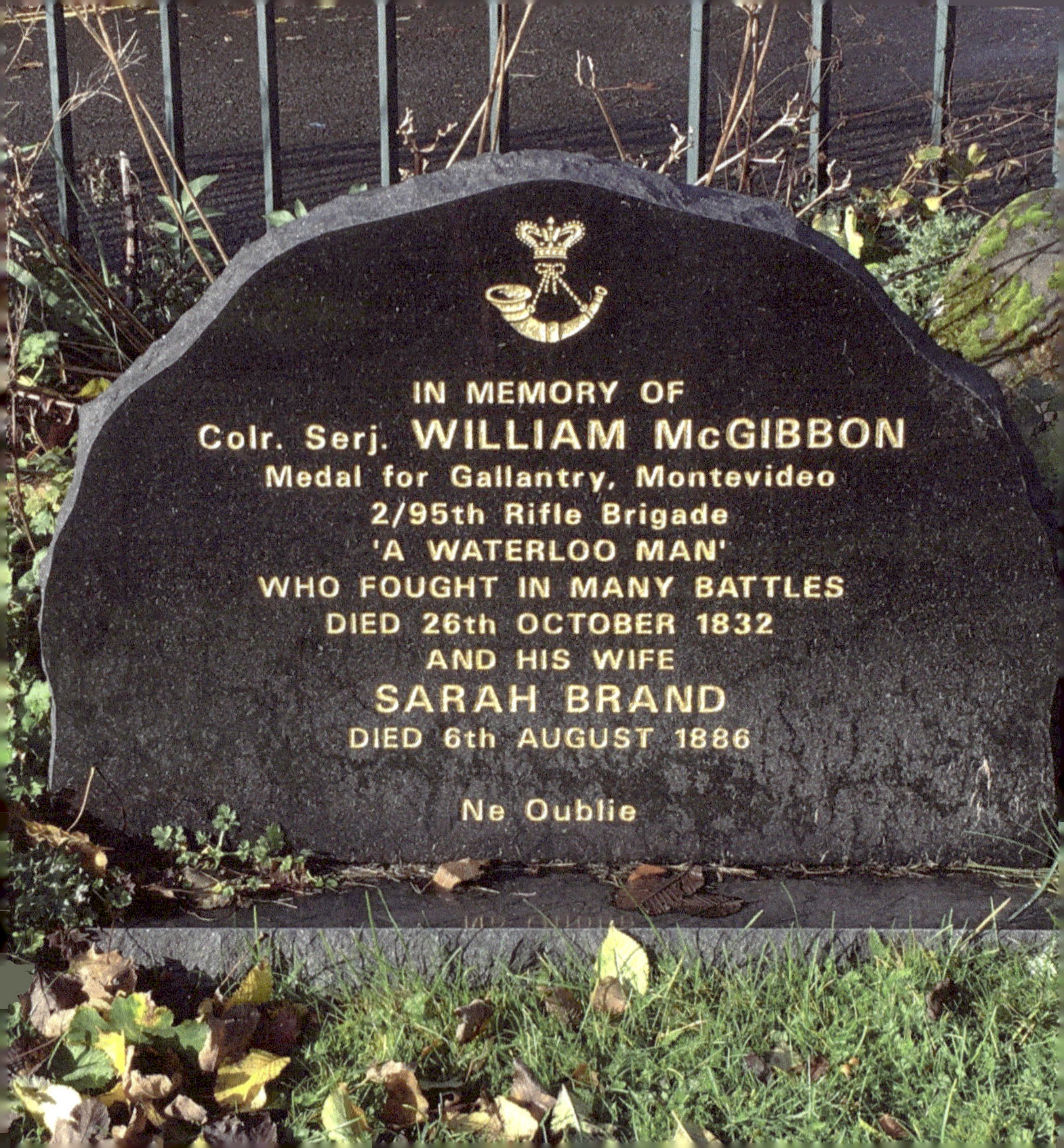
IN MEMORY OF
Colr. Serj. WILLIAM McGIBBON
Medal for Gallantry, Montevideo
2/95th Rifle Brigade
'A WATERLOO MAN'
WHO FOUGHT IN MANY BATTLES
DIED 26th OCTOBER 1832
AND HIS WIFE
SARAH BRAND
DIED 6th AUGUST 1886
Ne Oublie

William McGibbon

The Real Sharpe?

Of all the soldiers and heroes connected with Stirling, there is no more astonishing an individual than Colour Sergeant William McGibbon of the 2/95 Rifle Brigade: a green-jacketed rifleman made famous by Bernard Cornwall's *Sharpe* novels. These highly-skilled men fought with the longer range Baker Rifle as independent skirmishers.

We think William was from Stirling and at the Battle of the River Plate, Argentina in 1806–7, where he was awarded a medal for bravery at the storming of Montevideo against the Spanish. He was also involved in the badly-managed attack on Buenos Aires, where his unit took heavy casualties in severe street fighting before General Whitelocke surrendered—an action which led to his court-martial and dismissal.

William later fought under Ralph Abercromby in the 1809 ill-fated invasion of the Netherlands. Inevitably he ended up in the Peninsular War, fighting at the retreat of Corunna which saw the heroic death of General Sir John Moore whose father had been the Minister at the Church of Holy Rude as well as having been a Son of the Rock. William also fought at Fuentes d'Onoro and Badajos as well as Waterloo. The 2/95th was part of Clinton's Division of General Rowland 'Daddy' Hill's II Corps. At the crisis of the Battle, when Napoleon's Garde Imperiale advanced to attack the Allied centre, Wellington rode up and ordered the 2/95th forward to charge the French, who 'gave way'. This led to the retreat of the French Guard, the collapse of the French Army, and Wellington's most famous victory. William made it home, and remarkably died in his bed!

O'er the hills and o'er the main
Through Flanders, Portugal and Spain.
King George commands and we obey
Over the hills and far away.

William's grave is in the north-west corner of the Old Town Cemetery (NS 79081 93855).

Private Murphy

The Thin Red Line

Quite why Britain was fighting in the Crimea (1853–1856) is a complex matter, but ultimately it was aimed at stopping Russian aggression. In July 1853, Russia declared war on Turkey. France and Britain were drawn into the war in the context of considerable public support. France provided three-quarters of the troops for the expedition. The 93rd (Sutherland Highlanders), one of the predecessors of the Argyll and Sutherland Highlanders, fought at the ensuing Battle of Alma and helped drive the Russians back. There are several houses named Alma in Stirling, and we also gained two captured Russian cannon featuring double headed eagles, now to the side of Cowane's Hospital (37.2 NS 79184 93685).

The Battle of Balaclava is most widely remembered for the failed Charge of the Light Brigade. In the battle, the 93rd Sutherland Highlanders formed a three-deep line to cover a gap left by retreating Turks. They stood firm in this line, rather than in the more conventional square formation, to meet the Russian cavalry and drove them off; the first time a cavalry charge had been defeated by rifle fire. *The Times'* war correspondent William Russell described the soldiers as '*that thin red streak tipped with a line of steel.*' Matthew was one of the last survivors of the campaign. Another Thin Red Line survivor was General Sir John Alexander Ewart KCB, who commanded the 6th Company at Balaclava, and who we will hear more about later on. The famous check pattern of the A&SH echoes the Thin Red Line.

In the Old Town Cemetery, Private Matthew Murphy is buried to the north of the Church of the Holy Rude and to the South-west of Mars Wark (37.1 NS 79206 93734).

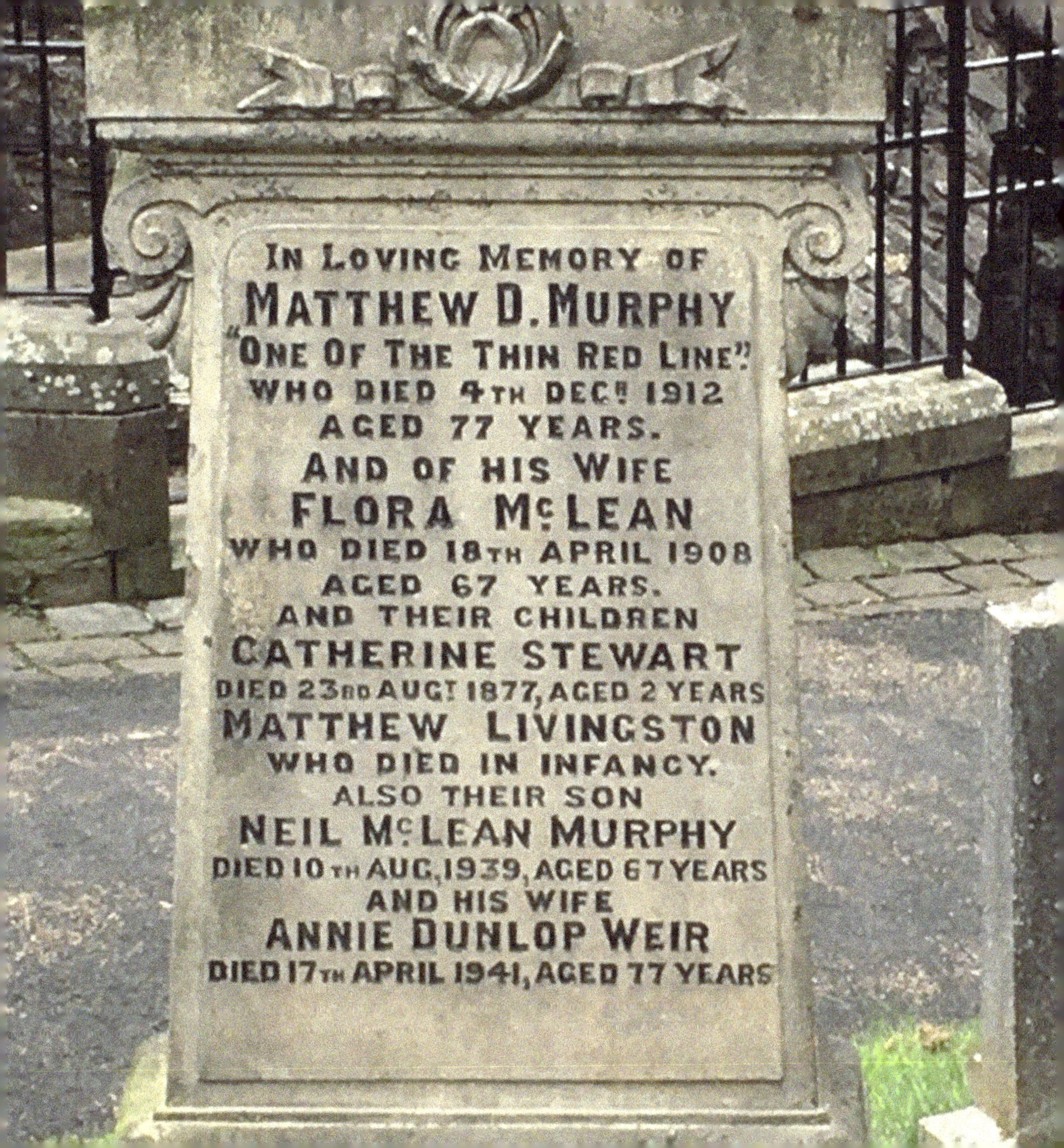
IN LOVING MEMORY OF
MATTHEW D. MURPHY
"ONE OF THE THIN RED LINE"
WHO DIED 4TH DECR 1912
AGED 77 YEARS.
AND OF HIS WIFE
FLORA McLEAN
WHO DIED 18TH APRIL 1908
AGED 67 YEARS.
AND THEIR CHILDREN
CATHERINE STEWART
DIED 23RD AUGT 1877, AGED 2 YEARS
MATTHEW LIVINGSTON
WHO DIED IN INFANCY.
ALSO THEIR SON
NEIL McLEAN MURPHY
DIED 10TH AUG, 1939, AGED 67 YEARS
AND HIS WIFE
ANNIE DUNLOP WEIR
DIED 17TH APRIL 1941, AGED 77 YEARS

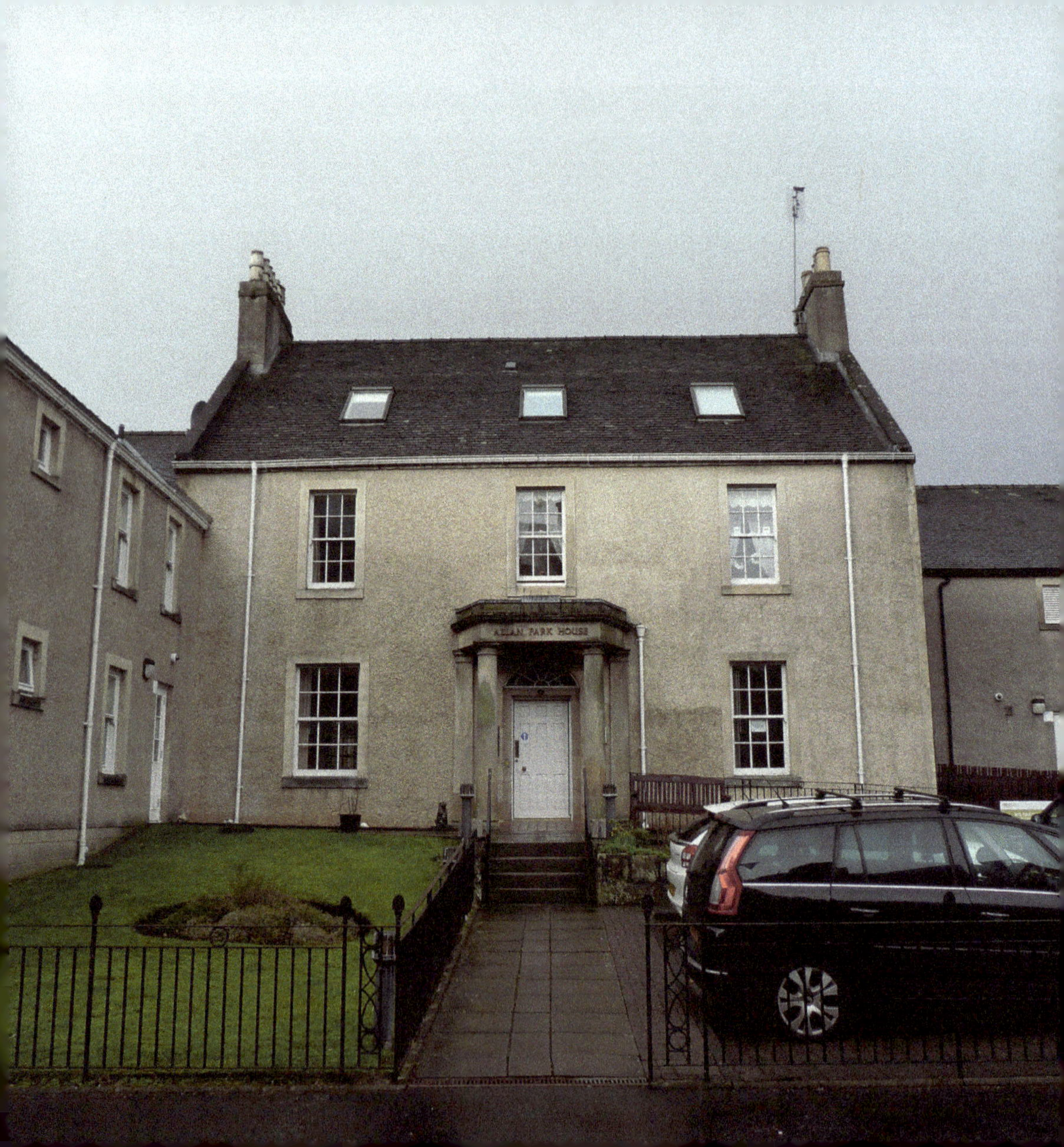
ALLAN PARK HOUSE

'The Indian Mutiny': Part 1
The Henderson Brothers MIA

This is not the place to debate or map the relationship of Britain and India; suffice it to say that while we talk of 1857 as 'The Indian Mutiny', they talk of the First Wars of Indian Independence.

At the time, India was a continent of different countries, ruled by Princes and Kings. The highest number of British people in India never exceeded 130,000, so British influence and control was exercised through these Princely States and by the commercial activities of the East India Company. There had always been resistance; the tragedy was that we divided them, and that Indians did most of the fighting and dying.

Our story concerns two young brothers from Allan Park, both teenagers when they left Scotland. Robert and John Henderson were ensigns in the 72nd and 56th Bengal Native Infantry respectively. Both were initially thought to have died in the chaos following the siege of Cawnpore in June 1856, where the soldiers were separated from the women and children. The soldiers were shot on the riverbank and only a few escaped including the Henderson brothers, whose fate was recorded by one of the survivors, Mowbray Thompson: Robert drowned trying to reach a boat, and his brother was shot in the hand and subsequently died. We might argue that such is the nature of war, but what happened next would turn anyone's stomach and was a clear and unambiguous war crime. The Indian troops massacred some 200 women and children a month later in July; it is unclear who gave the order.

Inevitably, this hardened attitudes to the Indians in Britain, and atrocities mounted on both sides. Lieutenant Colonel Neil ordered all villages besides the Great Trunk to be burnt and the villagers hanged. When Cawnpore was recaptured, the British took the Indian troops to the massacre and forced them to lick the blood from the walls and floor and then either hanged them or blew them from cannon. This, however, did not end the conflict.

The Henderson family memorial is located in the Old Town Cemetery to the north of the Guthrie statue (NS 79179 93795). The brothers are not buried here, and the location of their bodies remains unknown to this day.

'The Indian Mutiny': Part 2
The Relief of Lucknow

Britain's response to the 'mutiny' was overwhelming and included General Ewart, whom we heard of earlier during the Crimean Campaign. He took part in the second Relief of Lucknow, which is perhaps the quintessential episode of the British Empire. Whatever the rights and wrongs of the invasion, the besieged Britons and their relieving forces exhibited enormous bravery and courage under fire. Tennyson wrote of:

'Banner of England, not for a season, O banner of Britain, hast thou
Floated in conquering battle or flapt to the battle-cry!
Never with mightier glory than when we had rear'd thee on high
Flying at top of the roofs in the ghastly siege of Lucknow—
Shot thro' the staff or the halyard, but ever we raised thee anew,
And ever upon the topmost roof our banner of England blew.'

On the 29th June, the British population at Lucknow retreated into a cluster of buildings covering 60 acres. Here 855 British soldiers, 712 Indians, 1,451 civilians—including hundreds of women and children—were surrounded by 8,000 Indians. They held out for 87 days until the first relief came. This force lost 535 men out of 2,000, and then the siege lasted a further 61 days until 22nd November.

The final relief was led by the famous General Colin Campbell, and it was with this force that Ewart was involved. During the campaign his bonnet was shot off and he received two sword wounds leaving his arm in a sling, and then his left arm was shot off by cannon fire! He was recommended for a Victoria Cross for his role at Lucknow, but lost out in a vote. In total, six soldiers from the 93rd (the A&SH) won VCs at Lucknow. While we may debate why Britain was there in the first place, one cannot gainsay the military heroism, and Murray knows a Stirling man whose ancestor was rescued from Lucknow and would not be here today but for the relief.

General Sir John Ewart KCB, Colonel of Argyll and Sutherland Highlanders, is buried with his son Lieutenant Ronald Ewart in a modest grave at the north-east end of the Old Town Cemetery (NS 79208 93823).

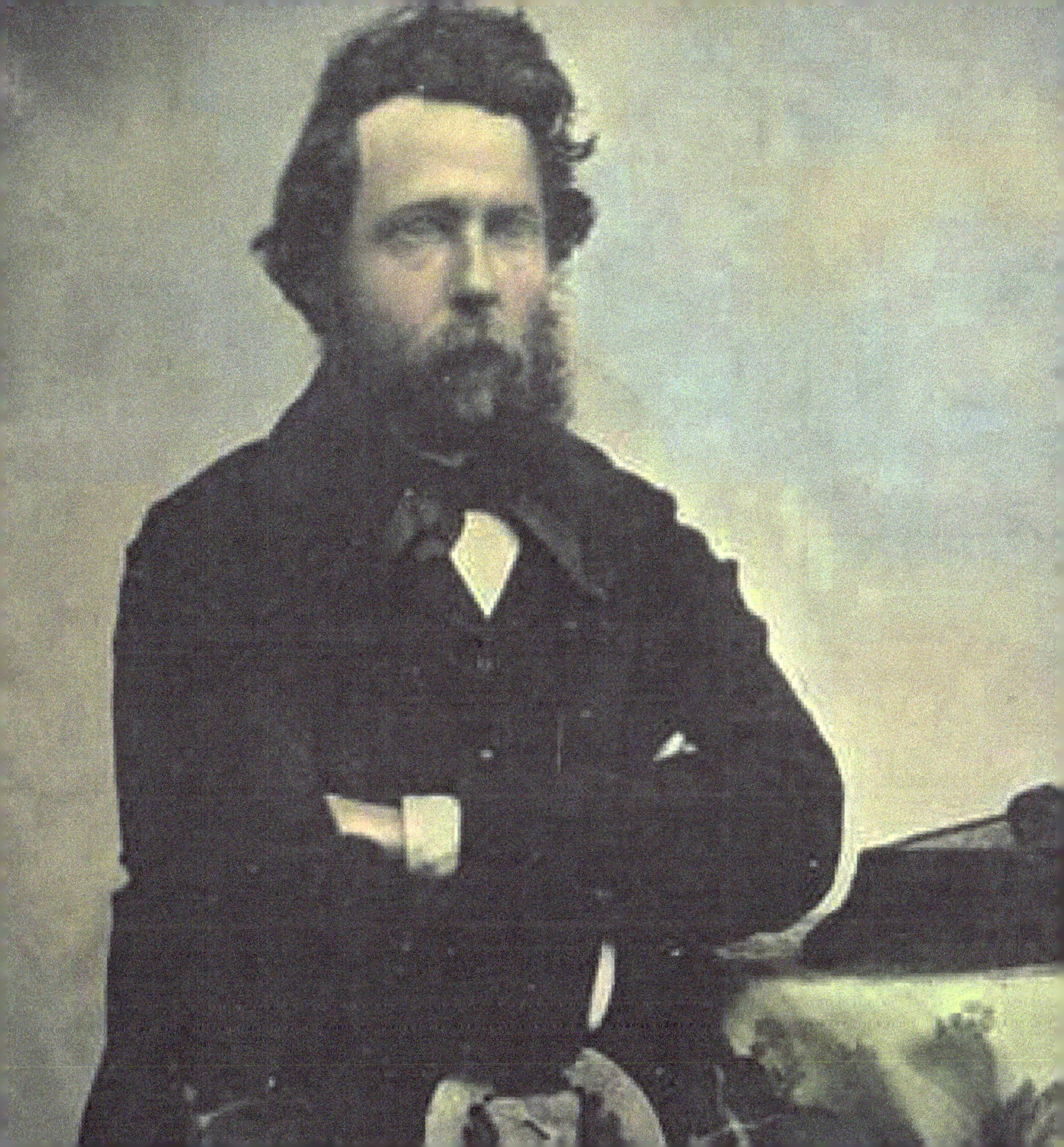

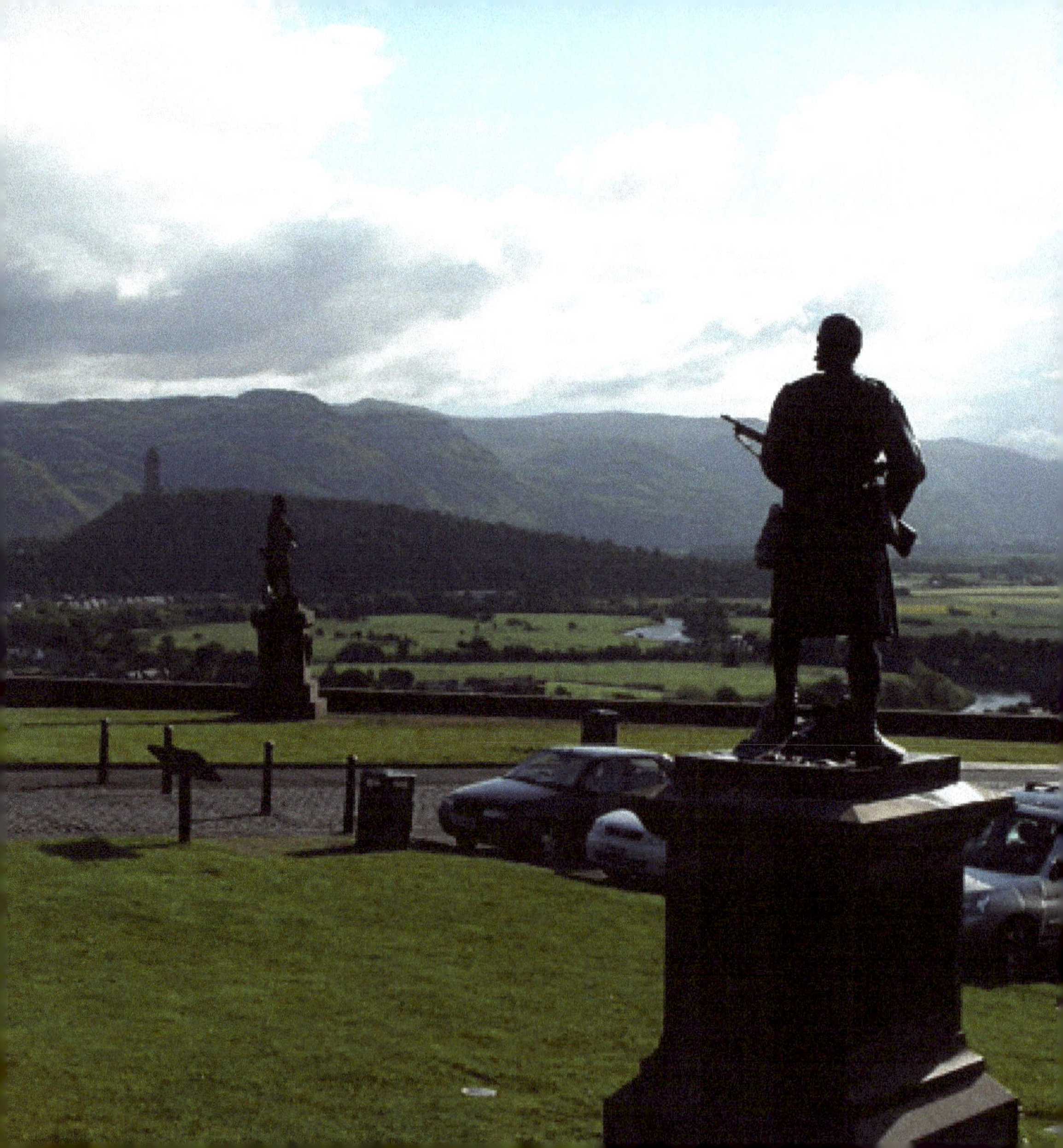

The Boer War

Gold, Death and 'Glory'

On 11 October 1899, the second South African War broke out after Britain rejected the Boer Republics' ultimatum to withdraw from their borders. Negotiations stalled over the rights of British gold prospectors. The Boers besieged Kimberley, Ladysmith and Mafeking and outfought the British throughout the conflict with a force of 45,000 irregulars repeatedly defeating significantly larger forces of up to 450,000. Major General Sir David Bruce (who went to Stirling High School) and his wife Mary ran the field hospital in Ladysmith during the 118 day siege. He is more famous for discovering the cause of Malta Fever, the Brucella virus, which is named after him.

A significant setback for the British was at Magersfontein, outside Kimberley. Here, the Highland regiments remained in close-order columns while fighting a concealed enemy armed with modern rifles and smokeless powder. These are similar to the circumstances that led to the death of Private Edmond Chissel at 21, in the advance to Brandfort on the 30th April. He and his comrades were trying to '*dislodge*' a number of Boers from a kopje (a small rocky hill). The term 'kop' made its way into British sports, with several football stadia having a sloped area known as 'the kop', after the Battle of Spion Kop.

The stiff Boer opposition led to a campaign aimed at denying them supplies. Farms and crops were burned, and the civilian population was concentrated into refugee camps. Soon disease and hunger led to increasing deaths, and these camps were widely criticised in the foreign press and in Britain. Eventually, 25,000 Boer women and children and at least 20,000 African workers died in these camps, from disease and incompetent management.

There are a number of monuments to The South African Campaigns round Stirling. One on the Castle Esplanade (40.1 NS 79093 93956) commemorates the Argyll and Sutherland Highlanders' role, and there is a small monument at Ladies Rock listing the dates of the sieges (40.2 NS 79117 93764). Major-General Sir David Bruce is buried in the cemetery (40.3 NS 79156 93762) as is Private Edmond Chissel (40.4 NS 79195 93752).

The Fighting Cocks
Barnwell, Liddell and 43 Squadron

Scotland's first powered flight was six years later than the Wright Brothers and took place in Causewayhead (41.2 NS 80526 95656), and by 1914 aircraft were fully engaged in World War 1. One of these early aviators was Aiden Liddell, the only Argyll VC winner to be commemorated with a brass plaque in the 'Regimental Kirk'—the Church of the Holy Rude. He was involved in the Christmas truce and won the Military Cross, before being wounded and invalided home. He was deemed to unfit for the trenches, but pushed to join the Royal Flying Corps (RFC). He was wounded on a recce mission in 1915, and kept the aircraft flying to save his observer. He would die of these wounds with his mother by his side on St Aiden's day, 31st August. According to a colleague, he was 'a fine Catholic gentleman'.

As the war progressed, 43 Squadron Royal Flying Corps was formed in April 1916 at Falleninch. Initially, the Squadron was equipped with the two-seater Sopwith 1½ Strutter biplanes in its role as photo-reconnaissance, but was converted to a Fighter/Ground Attack role in 1917. 43 Squadron suffered 35 flying casualties, from an original officer establishment of 32, as young replacements arrived and were shot down. The Squadron adopted the Fighting Cock emblem in 1926 and became the RAF's display squadron. In the Second World War, it was heavily involved in the Battle of Britain—flying Hurricanes—when they shot down 60 German aircraft, including the first enemy plane downed over England. Even during the jet age, the Squadron retained a cockerel as a mascot, and the most junior officer had to care for him. The Squadron standard is 'laid up' in the church of the Holy Rude. The motto *Gloria Finis* can be translated as 'Glory to the end.'

There is parking right next to the memorial, though it is tight (41.1 NS77840 93600).

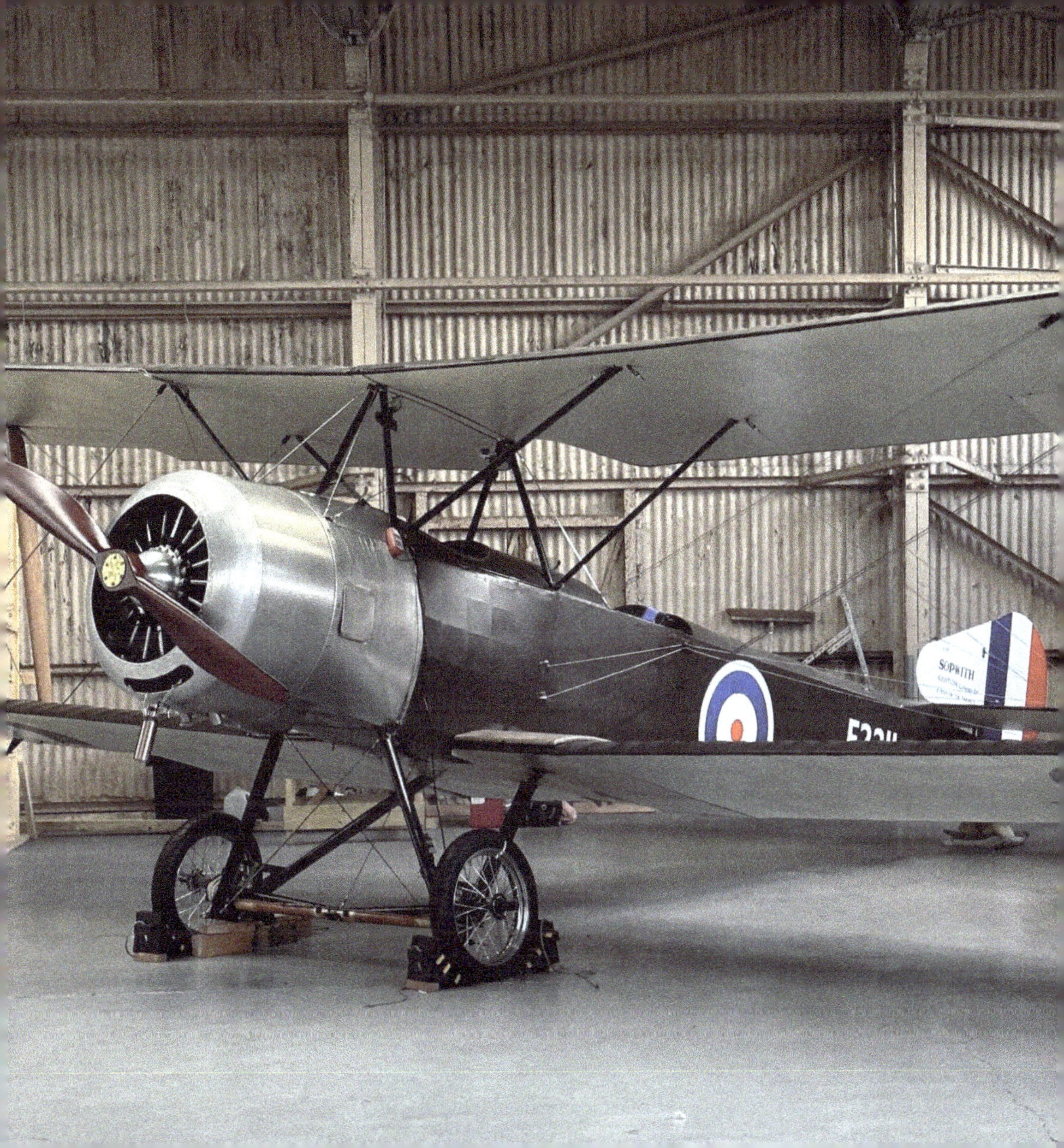
SOPWITH

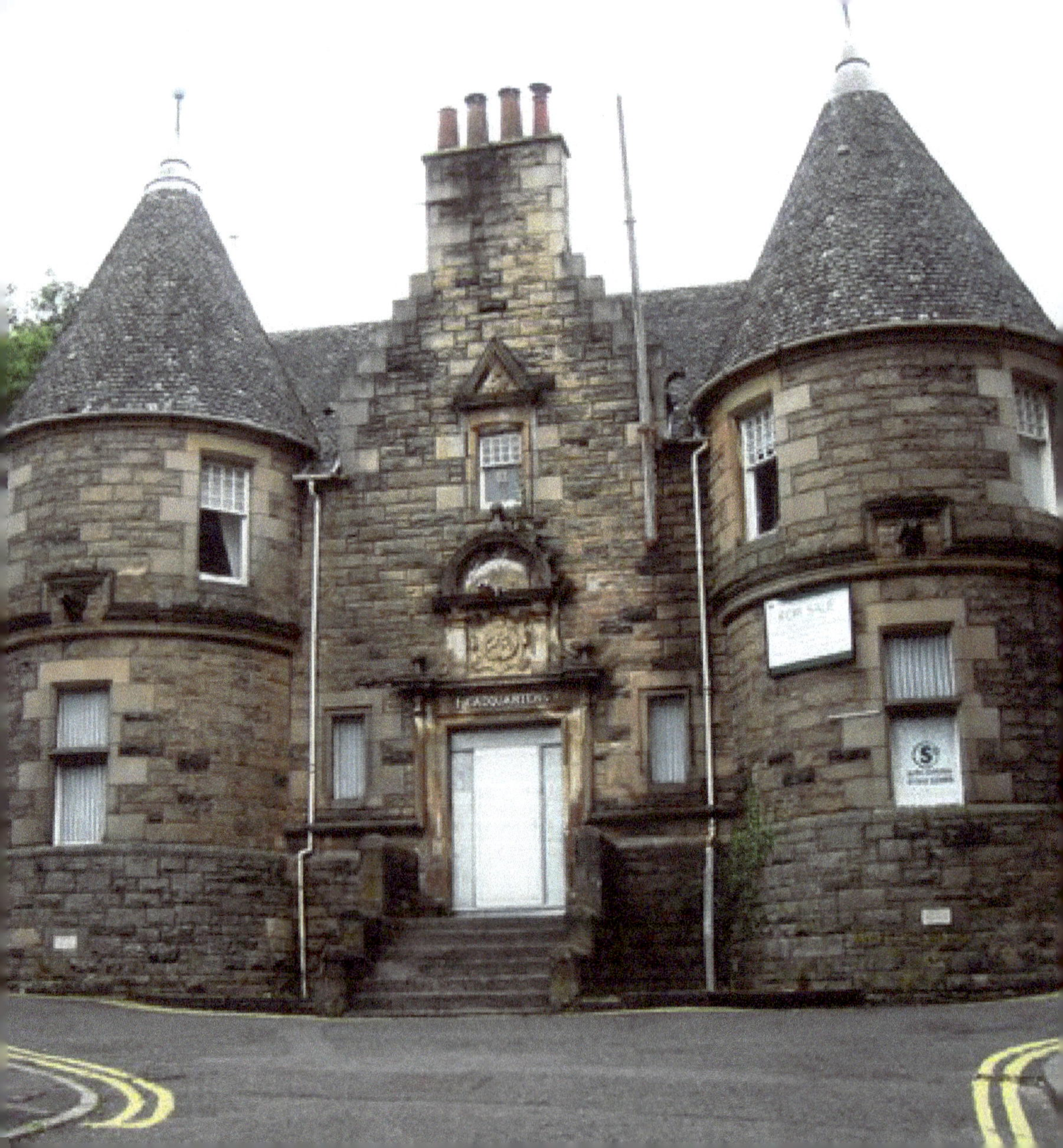

The Territorial Force

Stirling and the American Civil War

The Territorial Force was created from the Rifle Volunteer Movement, which had emerged in response to the threat of French invasion at the start of the 19th century. Interestingly, in Stirling they adopted uniforms which were almost identical to those worn by the Confederacy in the Civil War, suggesting popular support for the slave-owning Southern States. Certainly, the rebels sought to purchase fast, steam-powered blockade runners from the Clyde shipyards and established a headquarters in Bridge of Allan. Around ten agents were based there and helped with the purchase of 200 vessels.

The unlikely story still persists in the South that they were mostly descended from Scots, and that their tactics derived from the Highland charge. However, the Confederate Battle Flag was certainly based on the Saltire, and of course there is the Ku Klux Klan. Famously, Mark Twain blamed the savagery of the fighting on the mistaken ideals of honour promoted by Sir Walter Scott's novels, which of course also feature the burning cross favoured by the KKK. From the other side, William McCowan is commemorated outside Dunblane Cathedral (42.2 NN 78158 01357). A veteran, he died during training at Camp Readville as his regiment, the 58th Massachusetts, was being formed.

In Stirling, the Rifle Volunteers (RV) paid for their own equipment and were more like a Men's Club with guns (!), rather than a well-trained Army unit. They trained at the firing range at Falleninch, and metal detection by Murray found spent and impacted lead bullets across the path (42.3 NS 77996 93344). This had led to complaints by walkers! Over the years, the uniforms of these part-time volunteers were changed and, eventually, were very similar to those of the regular soldiers of the Argyll and Sutherland Highlanders.

At the top of Princes Street (42.1 NS 79474 93736) lies the Drill Hall, Headquarters of the 7th Battalion, (Princess Louise's) Argyll and Sutherland Highlanders.

Bandeath

Part of 'the most powerful naval fortress in the United Kingdom, and probably therefore, in the world.'

In 1916, the British Home Fleet was based at Rosyth in the Forth, and the above quote was by General George K Scott-Moncrieff. A key element of the network of defences was the huge complex of thirty-six magazine warehouses at Bandeath, in part built by German prisoners of war to be separated from the warships down-river. These magazines were all linked by a railway system which included a crane that could take supplies from the river. The largest of these shells stood as big as a man and weighed 879 kg.

In recent years, much of the smaller infrastructure has been removed including the concrete fire watchers' shelters. These were an integral part of the site, and each munition store contained the time required to walk to the nearest shelter in the event of a fire. Alan Wilson worked there in the early sixties and recalls that there was a complex of buildings outside 'The Explosive Area' featuring the canteen, dockyard supplies, fuel, etc. The entrance was marked by two gateposts of 15 inch shells, shined and painted. Alan handled shells, mines and 1,000lb aerial bombs, and that 'the gaffers had to cycle between the magazines'. The boss had a chauffeur-driven car and once arrived to congratulate Alan and his workmates for their rapid response in a fire drill.

After World War II there was a shortage of housing in Stirling, and 10 children aged between 1–15 slept on straw over a concrete floor at Bandeath. Others were turned away by Polish soldiers based there, and four adults and ten children walked until 4am to simply keep warm when they then snuck into an air raid shelter. The resulting evictions and prosecutions led 400 men to strike at the Plean pits in protest.

The Bandeath complex is accessed on foot via the modern industrial estate (NS 85164 91780), which also reuses military buildings. We do not recommend that you visit the crane, as it's in a very dangerous state.

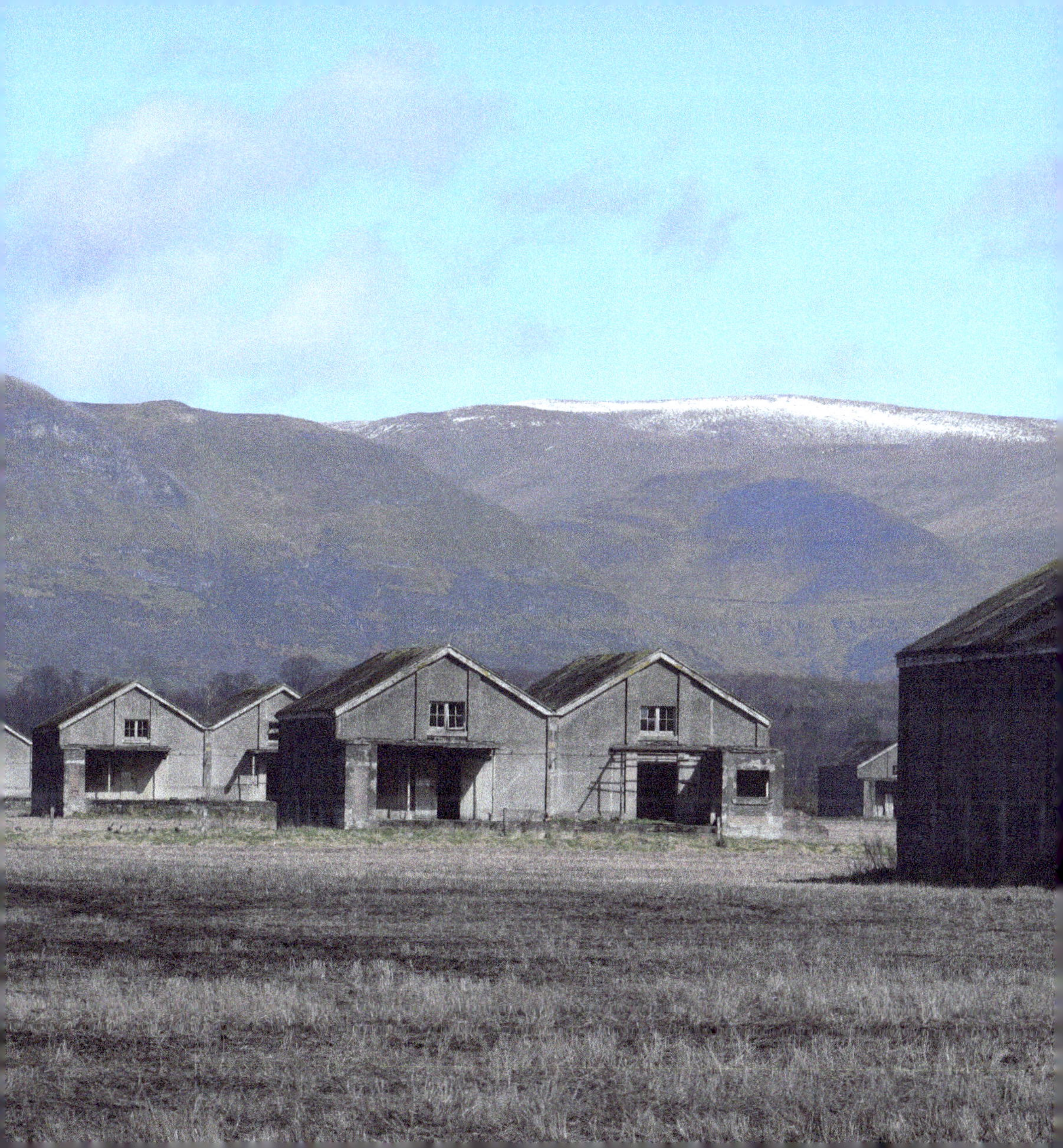

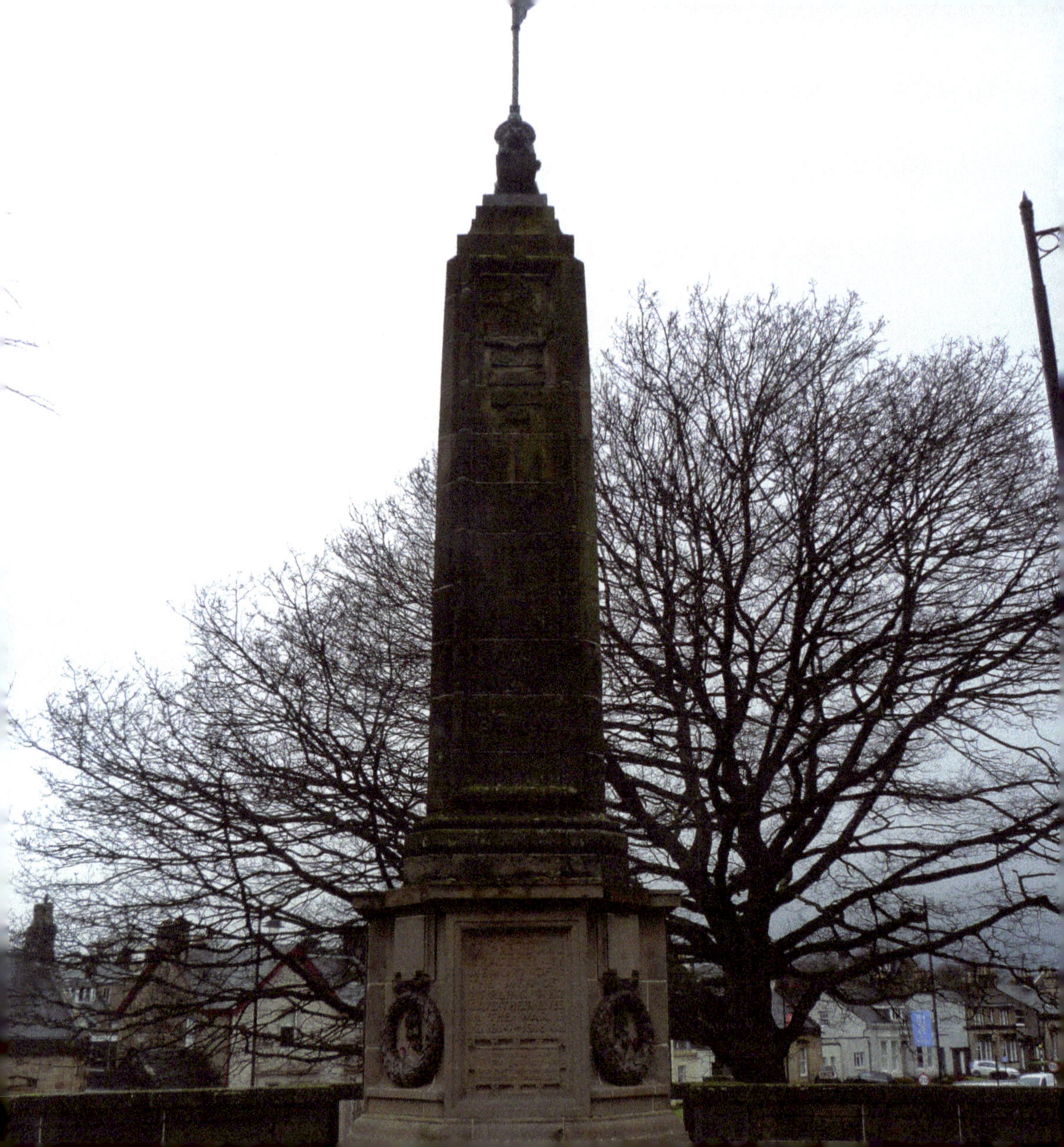

The Great War: Part 1
The King's Park

Stirling's 7th battalion of the Argyll and Sutherland Highlanders (about a thousand men) mobilised from the Princes Street Drill Hall in August 1914. As we've heard, these were local volunteers who would meet once a week for drill and socialising including an annual two-week camp, which for many was their only holiday. They were deployed to Bedford as part of the 51st Highland Division, to defend against a German invasion. 28,000 men in kilts arrived over a few days in a town of 30,000 inhabitants. Today, Bedford is proud of its connection to the Highland Division, and their kilted pipe-band marks each Remembrance Day, which is attended by the great-grandchildren of the men from Scotland who married locally when they returned from France.

Kitchener's successful 'Your Country Needs You' campaign led to large numbers of volunteers who were trained initially in Stirling Castle, but, as numbers increased, in tents in King's Park. A key element of this training was digging trenches which were in a zig-zag pattern so that any enemy shells would not blast all along a straight trench.

During the course of the war, the Regiment raised twenty-seven battalions and suffered over 7,000 dead. Their battles in 1914–18 are commemorated in a new stained glass window in the Holy Rude church. Stirling's dead are commemorated on the War Memorial (44.3 NS79475 93375).

Men who were destined to fight at Gallipoli are likely to have trained in King's Park, and were certainly billeted in Hayford Mills, Cambusbarron (44.4 NS 77569 92853). These troops were involved in Britain's worst ever rail crash on 22nd May 1915 at Quintinshill, where 226 people died. Finally, General Sir Ian Hamilton, who organised the disastrous Gallipoli Campaign, is buried at Doune (44.5 NN 71666 00692).

The King's Park practice trenches are only visible from the air (44.1 NS 79004 93039), though there are upstanding examples at Sheriffmuir (44.2 NN 83782 03670).

The Great War: Part 2
Private Cormick McChord: A True First World War Hero

Private Cormick McChord was already in his late 30s when he joined the 12th Battalion of the Argyll and Sutherland Highlanders in 1915. The 12th were a service battalion, and part of Kitchener's new army who were formed at Stirling in September 1914. It has been said that Britain fielded three armies: the Regulars, the Territorials and the New Army 'Service Battalions'.

On the 25th of October 1915, while helping Royal Engineers sappers to build a mine under German trenches, poison gas was released and the two sappers were overcome, so Cormick tied a rope to them and dragged them to the mine/tunnel shaft where he climbed up the ladder and then pulled the other two to safety. For this, he was awarded the Distinguished Conduct Medal. He stayed with the 12th for most of the war, until his wounds became so bad that he was invalided back to Britain for treatment. During this time, as part of his recovery he was selected to help make the altar front piece of St Paul's Cathedral. He is still commemorated as an Altar-man of St Paul's, and also commemorated in the 1920 book *Deeds that Thrill the Empire*.

After the war, Cormick decided to stay in Stirling where he moved into 17 Weaver Row, St Ninians, and stayed in the area until his death in 1946. He is survived by a very proud family who still live in Stirling.

There is ample parking for Bannockburn Cemetery where Cormick (NS 81293 90586) is buried, and we are indebted to Eric Thornton who compiled this entry.

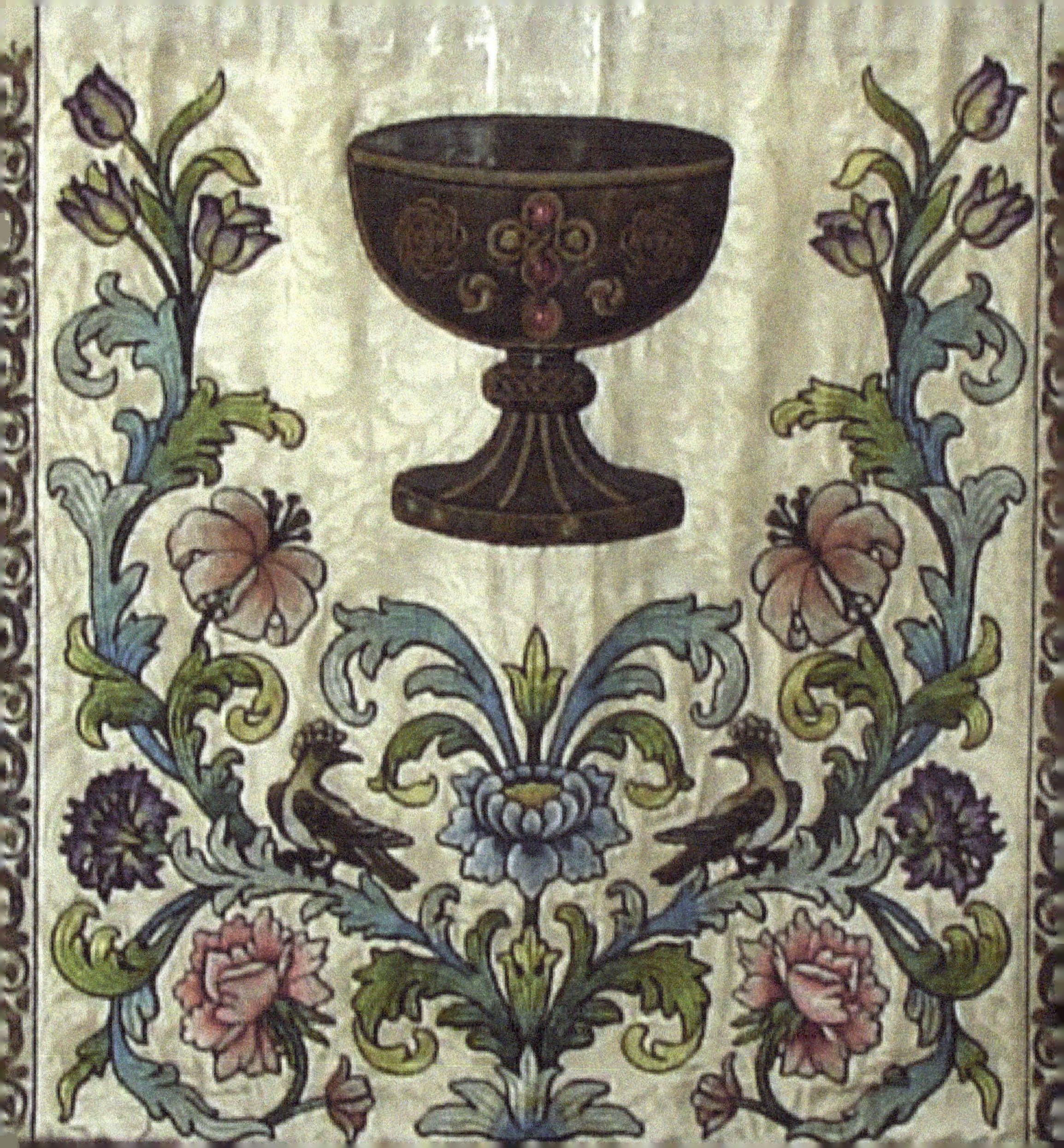

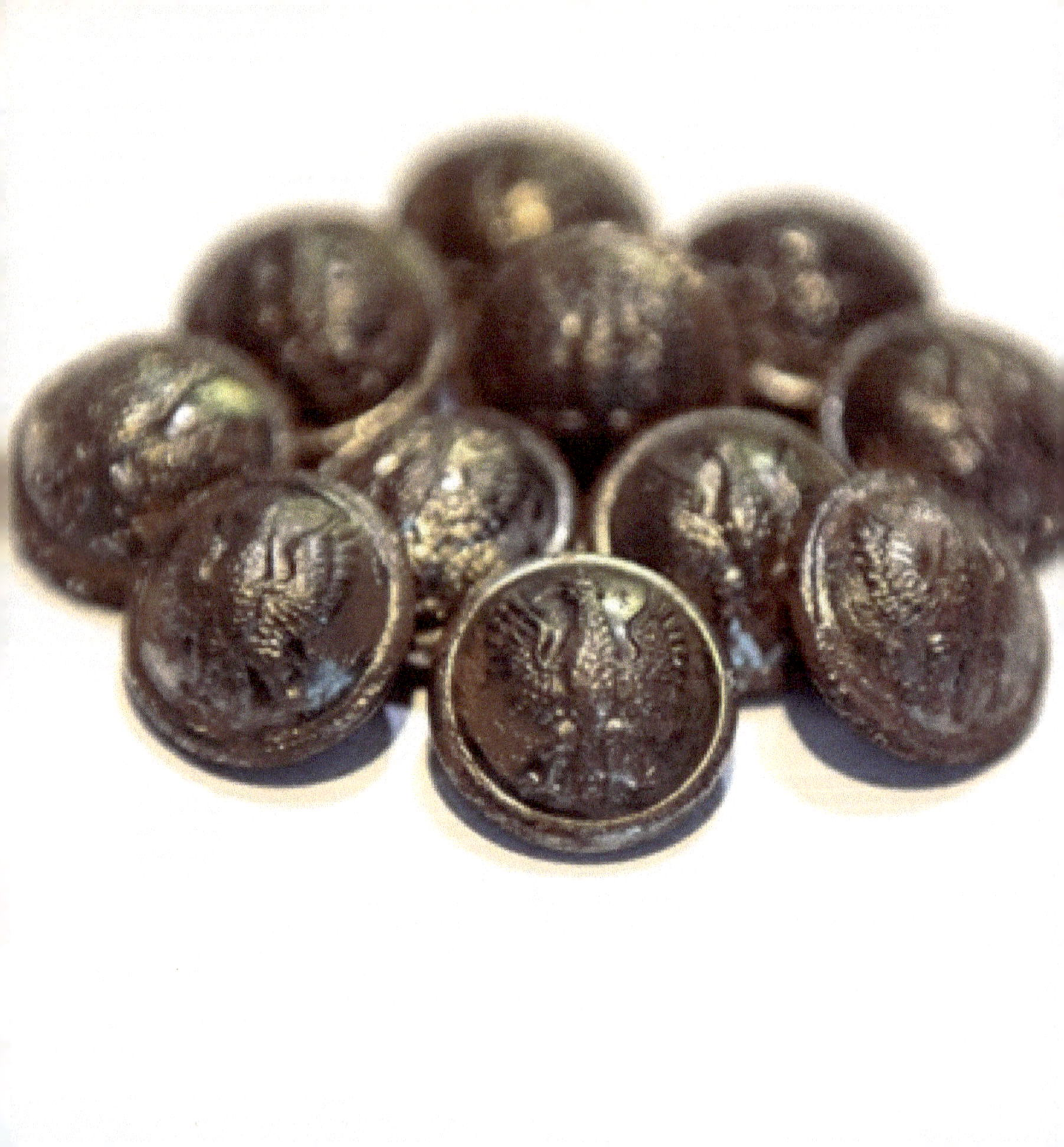

The Second World War: Part 1
Polish Troops

Following the joint German and Russian invasion of Poland in September 1939, what remained of the free Polish army and Government moved first to France and then to Britain to continue the fight. 20,000 Polish soldiers were spread across Britain to help strengthen strategic defences. In due course, they were joined by free forces from across Europe eager to continue the fight.

While some Polish troops were based in existing buildings like Bridge of Allan Museum, there were simply too many of them and many ended up in Nissen Huts; there are several clusters round Stirling—all surviving as concrete bases, though there are upstanding examples at Cultybraggan near Comrie (46.1 NN 76918 20041). The most accessible are at the King's Knot (46.2 NS 78956 93857), while the most impressive are a line that run down the wooded ridge north of Well Road, Bridge of Allan (46.3 NS 79309 97598). These structures were hot in summer and cold in winter!

In Dunblane, there was a heavy machine gun battalion and they helped at a military hospital. We think the area round the modern Hydro was used for training. It was in this area that local metal detectorist Jude Maxwell found several double-headed eagle buttons. These are from a Polish uniform made in the early 1940s when the troops were reorganised into divisions and the UK provided training, clothing and equipment. This many buttons implies that they were lost together. Quite how they ended up in a field near the Hydro is unclear; perhaps a jacket blew off a washing line and rotted away, or maybe the buttons were cut off as a memento and then lost. However the buttons ended up in Dunblane, it is worth reflecting on those brave men and women who continued to fight for freedom. Poles fought at Monte Cassino, and the Polish parachute brigade were flown from Scotland to be dropped at Arnhem as part of Operation Market Garden (The Bridge Too Far?). In addition, the famous Polish Armoured Division moved from Scotland to Normandy and was the key unit in closing the Falaise Gap and defeating the Germans. Scandalously, the Poles were denied a role in the 1945 Victory parade for fear of upsetting the Soviets.

The Second World War: Part 2
The Home Guard

This is not the place to debate the history of the Home Guard and its evolution from Local Defence Volunteers or the complex issues raised by arming and training civilians who then might become enemy combatants if the German invasion succeeded. The Home Guard combined multiple aims, from morale boosting to protection of industrial assets. It also included secret units who were to wage war in a last-ditch mixture of sabotage, collaborator assassination and guerrilla war in the event of a German invasion. They had secret bases and received no formal public recognition.

Metal detection by Murray across the Abbey Craig and Gowan Hill (47.1 NS 79192 94271) has recovered spent rifle shells from the early 1940s, presumably used in training by the Home Guard, although perhaps simply from infantry training. Firmer evidence comes from northern and western slopes of Abbey Craig, where there is a series of small stone shelters used as training positions (47.2 NS 81005 95635).

A possible example of the Home Guard's proposed guerrilla war is on the road from Bridge of Allan, which in places is very narrow and gorge-like. Here there are two sets of iron rail tracks cemented into the road (47.3 NS 80502 97106) which were spotted by Gordon Wilkie. These were presumably designed to block the road by placing iron bars or trees or logs in order to hamper enemy troop movements. But might we imagine an even more desperate tactic where a section or a column of German troops was trapped between the two positions and then attacked from above?

It's not clear when this was built, but there was a wave of road blocks constructed in early 1940 by local Home Guards. However, by December the situation changed completely and *Scottish Command Operation Instruction No.2* ordered that no more roadblocks were to be built as they might hamper any British counter attack.

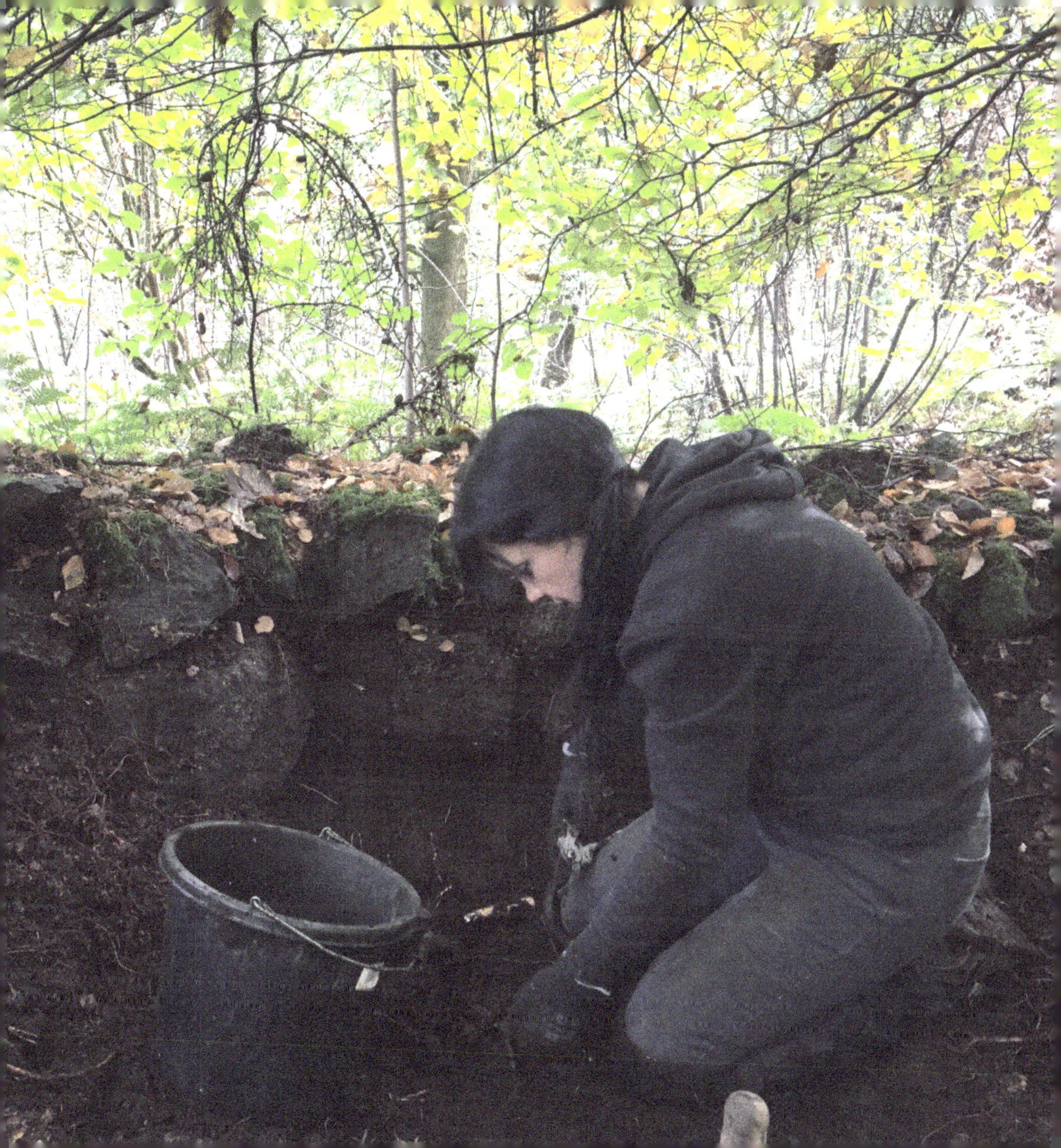

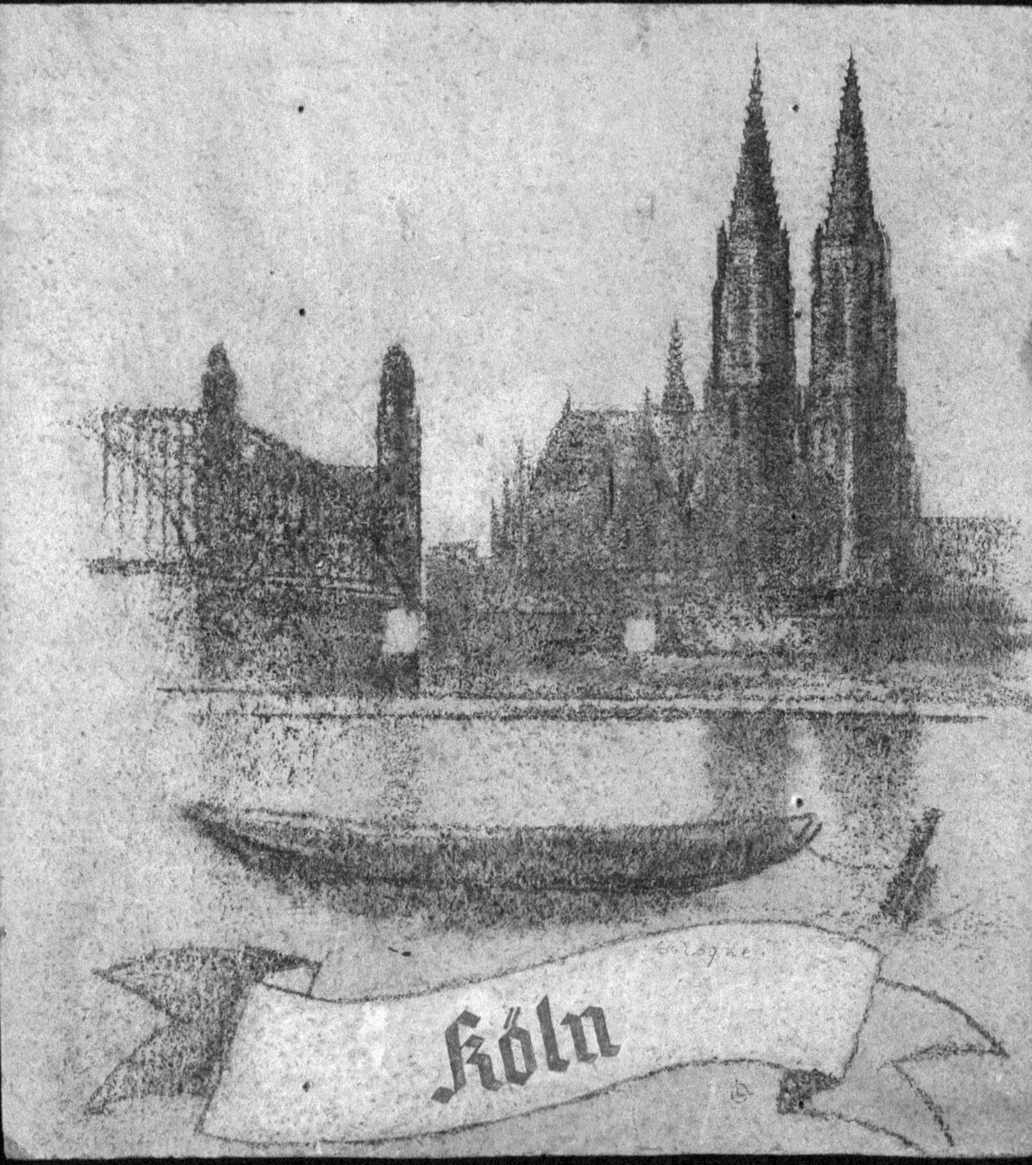

Cologne.
Köln

The Second World War: Part 3
Prisoners of War

Dramatic British victories in North Africa led to an Italian collapse and the capture of many prisoners. Castlerankine, Denny—comprising 39 huts—was one of the earliest camps to be built to hold these Italian prisoners (Camp 64) (48.3 NS 79302 81898). To this day, the locals refer to this Italian Camp as the 'Tahlly Camp'. These young Italian men were popular with the local girls. Indeed, a prudish letter to the *Falkirk Herald* in August 1944 complained about '*disgusting and shameful conduct*' with young girls and '*married women who come from far and near in crowds*' to meet prisoners by appointment, noting that '*the disgraceful conduct that takes place quite openly is disgusting*'.

Following D-Day in June 1944, increasing numbers of Germans were captured and by 1946, 2,100 were held in Camp 64. Artwork produced by prisoner Otto Laub using boot polish is displayed in the Stirling Smith Museum and Art Gallery (48.4 NS 79091 93519). Camp 559 occupied a more surprising location and was established on the slope above Causewayhead in the grounds of Abbey Craig House (which is not open to the public), where the large south-facing garden was filled with Nissen huts.

At Aberfoyle, Camp 593 (48.4 NN 53150 00150) was designated as Rob Roy. This is the location of today's Rob Roy Hotel. Interestingly, many Prison Camps were converted into holiday camps and low-cost hotels following the war: think Butlins or *Hi-De-Hi*!

The best example of a Prisoner of War Camp around Stirling is at Cultybraggan near Comrie (48.1 NN 76918 20041). This was one of the most secure camps in Britain and, towards the end of the war, housed the most fervent Nazis.

The Second World War: Part 4
The Special Air Service

The SAS was formed in 1941 in Africa's North Western Desert, following a failed parachute jump by David Stirling. He chose the motto 'Who Dares Wins'. The unconventional unit was not popular with the Regular Army, and Stirling had difficulty arranging the supplies and support he needed. When Churchill was visiting, he insisted that Stirling be invited to a wine-fuelled dinner. Towards the end, Stirling passed a napkin to Churchill asking him and the other important guests to sign it as a memento. Later he added the text *'Please give David Stirling Every Assistance'* above their signatures, and then got all the help he needed. Following Stirling's capture and imprisonment in Colditz, the SAS was commanded by an Irishman, Paddy Mayne, who won three DSOs, was denied the VC, and personally destroyed more German aircraft than any RAF pilot!

The SAS, or Sassmen as they called themselves, fought through Sicily and Italy, and their wartime dead are commemorated at the David Stirling statue. Returned to Britain, the SAS prepared for D-Day where their mission was to disrupt German supply lines. On one of the missions was Lieutenant Leslie Cairns from Doune. In 1944, Cairns (aged 24) was a member of D Squadron, under the command of Major Ian Fenwick. The Squadron was parachuted into various locations around Orleans, well behind the Normandy beachhead, as Operation Gain. Unfortunately, Leslie and the fifteen men he commanded—along with the crew of six airmen—never made it and they were posted missing, presumed killed on 18th June 1944. Leslie is commemorated on both the Bayeux Commonwealth War Memorial in France as well as in Snowdon Cemetery, below Stirling Castle (49.2 NS79067 93921).

There is ample parking at the David Stirling memorial (49.1 NN 75284 00369), which was built on land from his former family estate.

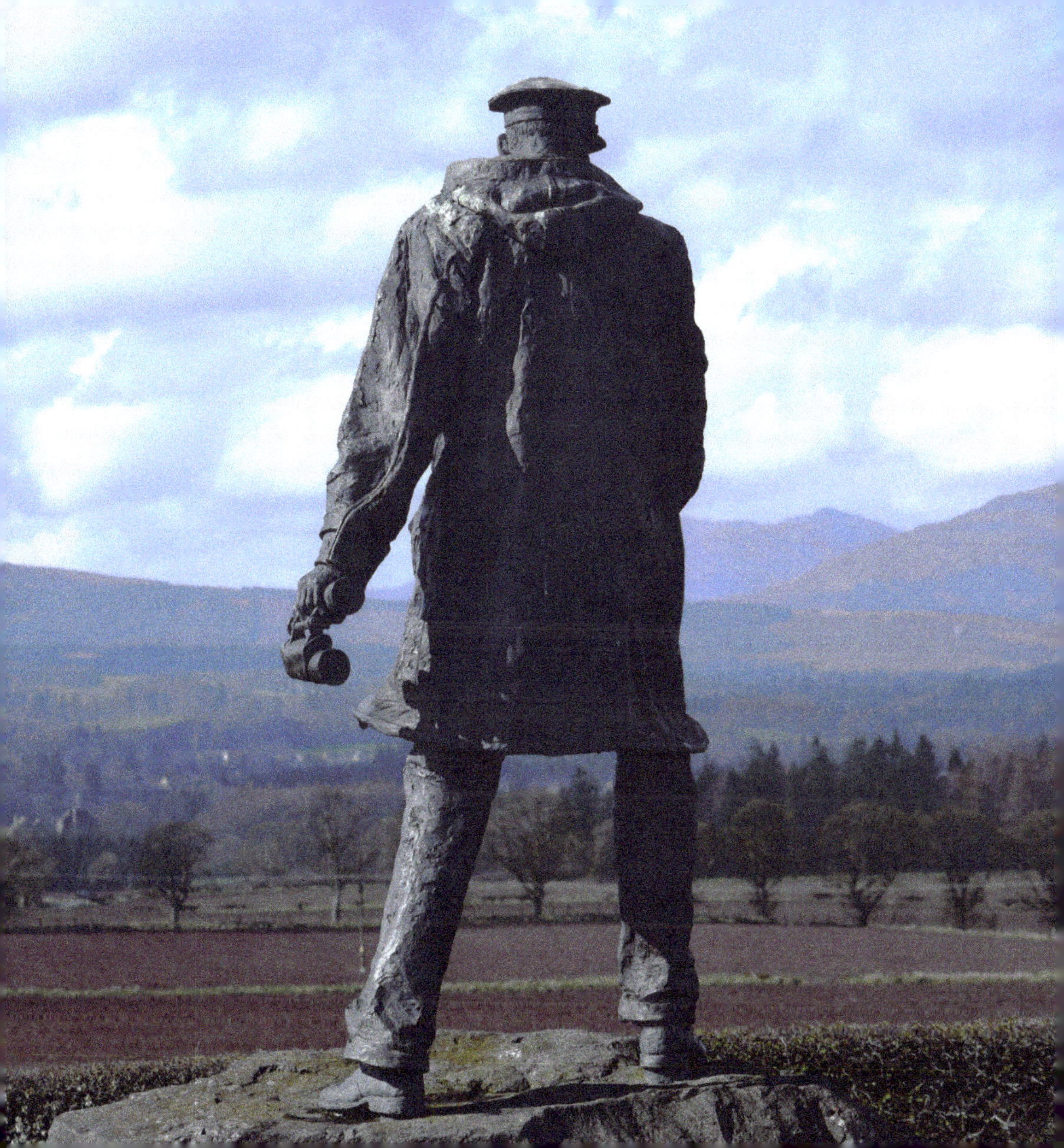

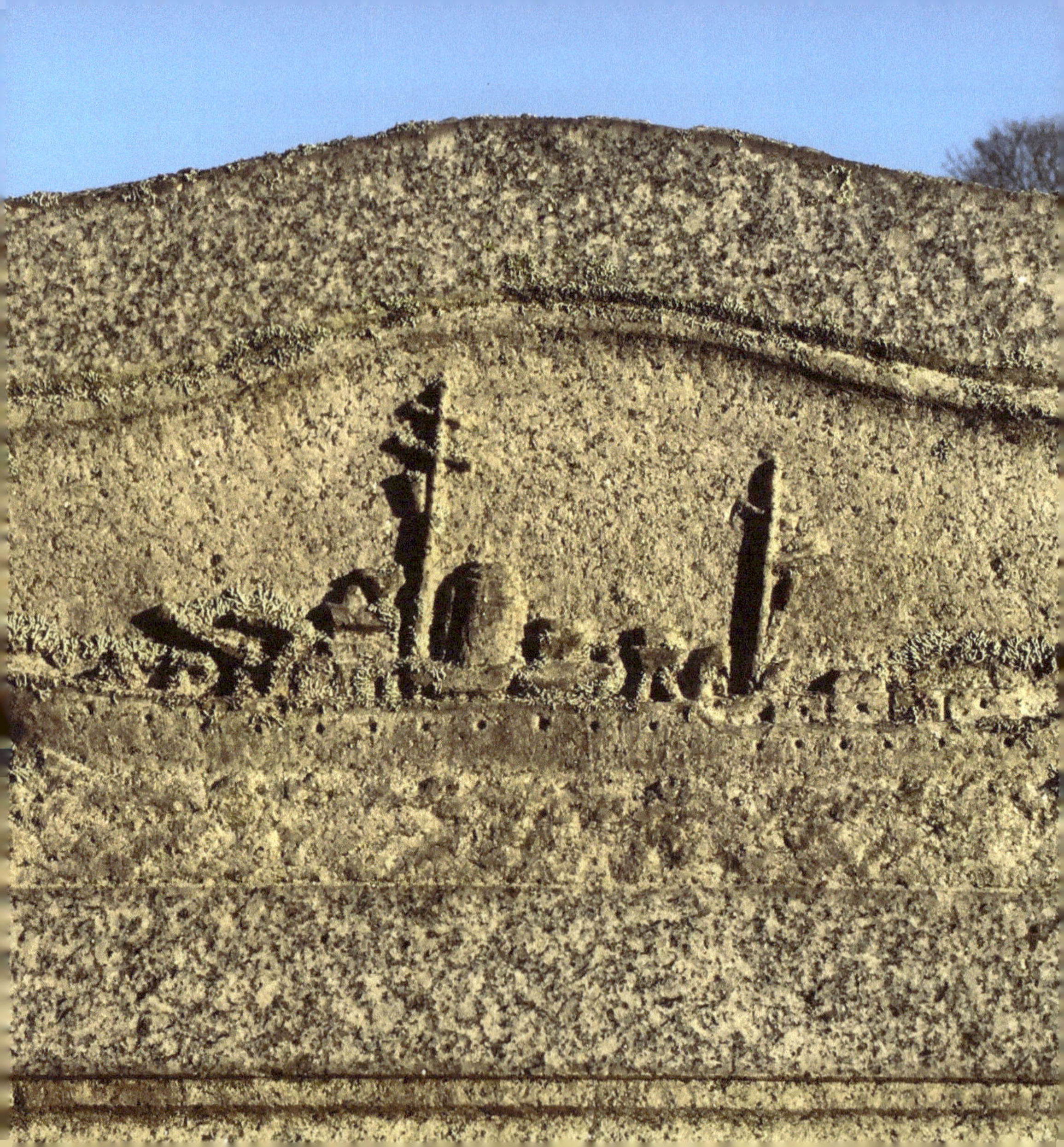

The Second World War: Part 5

The Arctic Convoys

War makes for strange bedfellows. In 1939, Hitler and Stalin secretly agreed to divide Poland between them. While the German atrocities in Poland are well known, the Soviets also murdered 22,000 Polish officers and civic leaders at Katyn, and took the larger part of Poland to themselves. The Soviets also provided the fuel which was used by the Luftwaffe in the German raids on Clydebank and in the south-east of England during the Battle of Britain.

Following the German invasion of Russia in 1941, Stalin turned to the Allies. Britain began a series of convoys through Arctic waters to keep Russia supplied. 78 convoys of over 1,400 merchant ships braved the frozen journey, their route started in Loch Ewe and battled against terrible weather and German attacks from air and submarine. The men received little thanks from the Russians when they arrived in Murmansk and were only formally recognised by Britain in 2012 with the Award of the Arctic Star campaign medal. Eighty-five merchant vessels and sixteen Royal Navy warships were lost in these efforts to supply the Soviet Union. Britain supplied almost half of the tanks in their victorious Battle for Moscow in 1941.

Malcolm 'Bunty' McPhee McColl (D/KX 178587) was the son of Malcolm and Margaret McColl of Stirling. Bunty (an affectionate name for someone who was small and plump) was a stoker on the HMS *Mounsey* (K 569), which was escorting Convoy RA-61 of 37 merchant ships. She was damaged by a torpedo fired from the German submarine U-295, which killed ten sailors. *Mounsey* was forced into the Kola Inlet for temporary repairs before returning to Britain. Bunty died at 21 in a frozen November of 1944 along with nine other sailors, leaving his wife Annie a widow. He is commemorated on the family tombstone which has a carving on HMS *Mounsey* at the top.

The memorial to Malcolm 'Bunty' McPhee McColl is in Stirling's Snowden Cemetery (NS 79029 93929).

The Second World War: Part 6
D-Day Preparations: 'The End of the Nazis Started Here'

Stirling Castle was a key training centre for the Highland Regiments. As part of the planning for D-Day and the liberation of France, replicas of the German Atlantic defences (built on the continent using slave labour) were constructed on Sheriffmuir from plans smuggled out of occupied Europe in a biscuit tin. Soldiers practised leaving 'landing craft' and charging across the grassy 'beach' under fire from enemy artillery and machine guns. The wall is 86m in length from NE to SW, and stands to about 3m in height with a flat-bottomed anti-tank ditch to its front.

The main purpose of the replica, however, was to work out how to blow the concrete up, and none of the soldiers who trained here was involved in the Normandy landings! However, that quote from the title is from Professor Tony Pollard about the significance of the replica. That being said, this concentration of troops provided another opportunity. Stirling Castle played a key role in Operation Fortitude North, which created a huge fictitious 'Fourth Army' ready to invade Norway. The HQ of the non-existent II Corps was Stirling Castle. From here, radio and other signals were sent to create the impression that 180,000 soldiers were based in the area, ready to invade Norway; there were even BBC announcements of fake inter-unit football scores within II Corps. In addition, both President Eisenhower and the exiled Norwegian King Haakon VII made speeches asking the Norwegian resistance not to act too soon.

The Germans maintained a garrison of half a million soldiers in Norway. None were moved south to oppose the Normandy landings (the largest amphibious invasion ever mounted). This was all thanks to a small planning staff and a few mobile signallers, pretending to be the headquarters of large forces.

There is limited parking on the side of the road and you will need welly boots. The surface is very uneven, and the wall has iron rebar sticking out (NN 83782 03670).

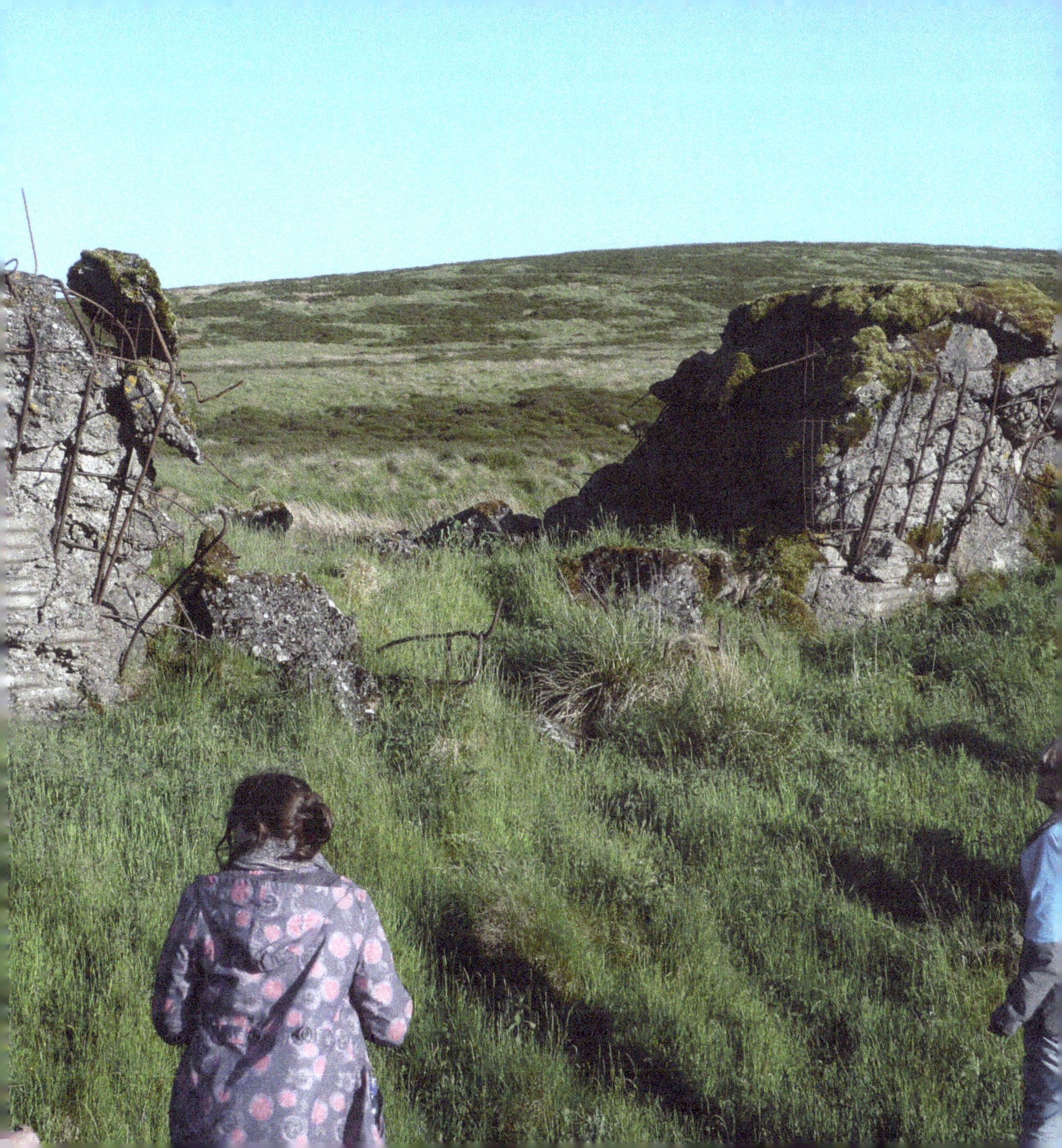

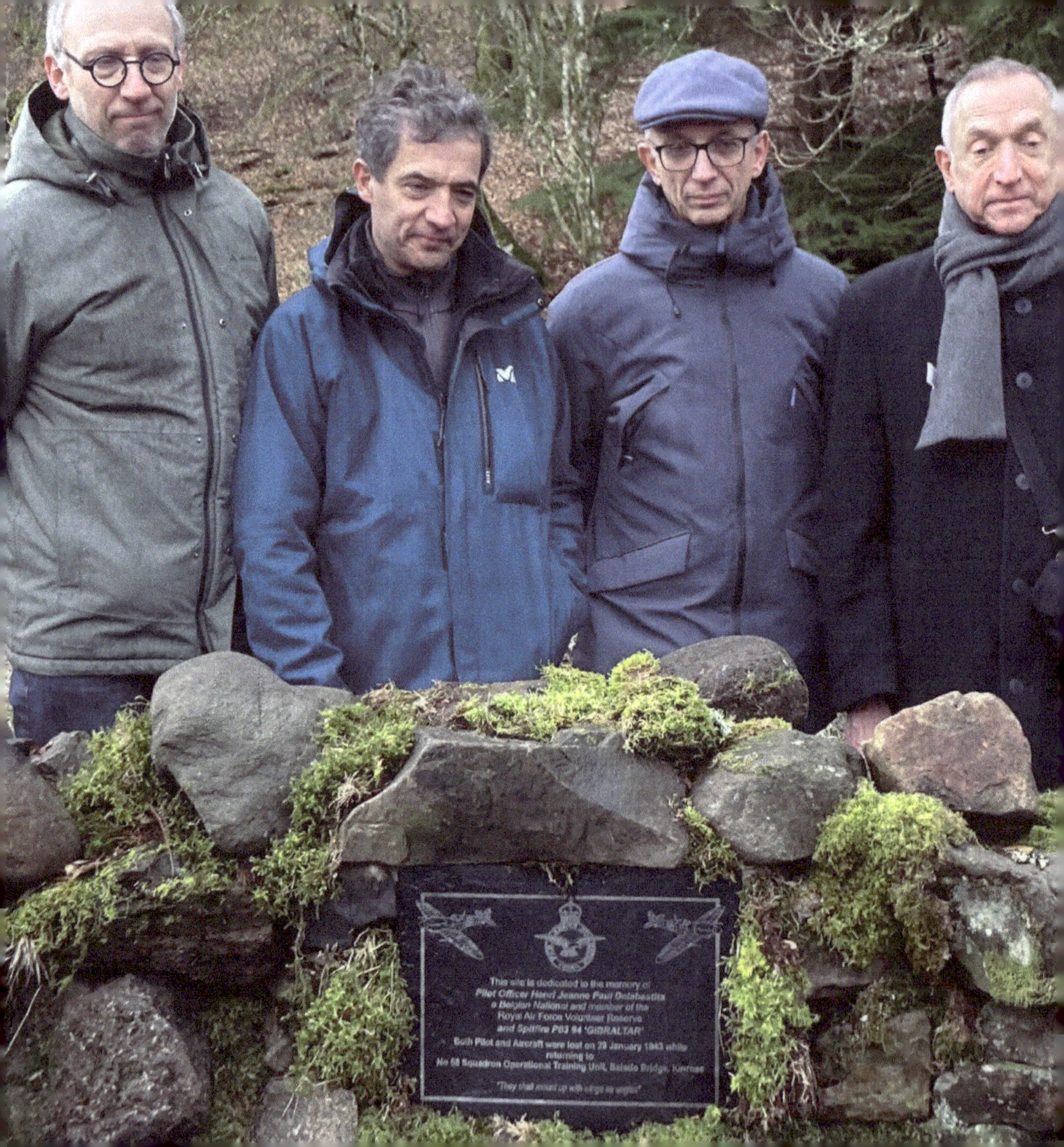
This site is dedicated to the memory of
Royal Air Force Volunteer Reserve
'GIBRALTAR'
Both Pilot and Aircraft were lost on 29 January 1943 while
returning to

The Second World War: Part 7

Crash Sites

Stirling District is dotted with Second World War crash-sites, mostly from accidents associated with trainee Spitfire fighter pilots from No.58 Operational Training Unit, based in Grangemouth. Pilots were taught basic skills in a Tiger Moth and then a more powerful two-seater Harvard before transferring to an OTU and the much more powerful single-seat Spitfire. Seventy-one pilots from 58 OTU died and are commemorated with a replica Spitfire and memorial wall, to the north of the site of the airfield on the A904, in Grangemouth. Many of these pilots are buried in Grandsable cemetery, Grangemouth, where we find the resting places of those young men whose bodies were not sent home: Canadian, Polish, Australian, New Zealand, Dutch, Czech and other graves (52.2 NS92425 79338).

The stories of two of these heroes are worth looking at in detail. Pilot Officer Carlyle Gray Everiss from New Zealand was practising dog-fighting skills when his Spitfire went into a spin and crashed on the railway embankment north-west of Cowie. Villagers believed that he stayed at the controls to avoid hitting a row of houses, and he has a personal memorial in the village (52.3 NS 83473 88968).

The second story concerns Henri Jeanne De La Bastita. Henri was a 37 year old Belgian national who had first fought with the Belgian air force before being captured by the Germans. He somehow made it to Britain and joined the RAF Volunteer Reserve. He appears to have blacked out due to oxygen failure and his Mk II Spitfire 'Gibraltar' (P8394) crashed in North Third on 29th January 1943. Murray and Jim were involved in the creation of a memorial to Henri at the crash site, which was unveiled by his nephews on 29th January 2023.

Henri De La Bastita's memorial is a five minute walk from the main road, but the path is uneven and muddy (52.1 NS 75679 88069).

The Second World War: Part 8

The War with Japan and the Death Railway

A key strategic aim of the Imperial Japanese in World War 2 was the connection of their conquered territories. Between what was then Siam (Thailand) and Burma (Myanmar), the Japanese planned a railway which was to be built by both prisoners of war and civilian forced labour. The project cost between 80,000 and 100,000 lives, including over 12,000 prisoners of war; as with all wars, civilians did the bulk of the suffering, hence its nickname 'The Death Railway'.

The men of the Second Battalion of the Argylls were taken prisoner as part of the surrender at Singapore, along with other soldiers, sailors and airmen. They became forced labour at the Death Railway, and almost 200 men died before final victory. A local man forced into this slave labour was Leading Aircraftman Robert Nicholas Shaw, who died while working on the railway on the 11th November 1943 at the age of 23. That is I'm afraid all we know of Robert. He is commemorated at Ballengeich cemetery. One final notice about Robert is that he never knew his father, another Robert, who died from his wounds before his son was born.

Robert Shaw's memorial is in Stirling's Ballengeich Cemetery (NS 79082 94202).

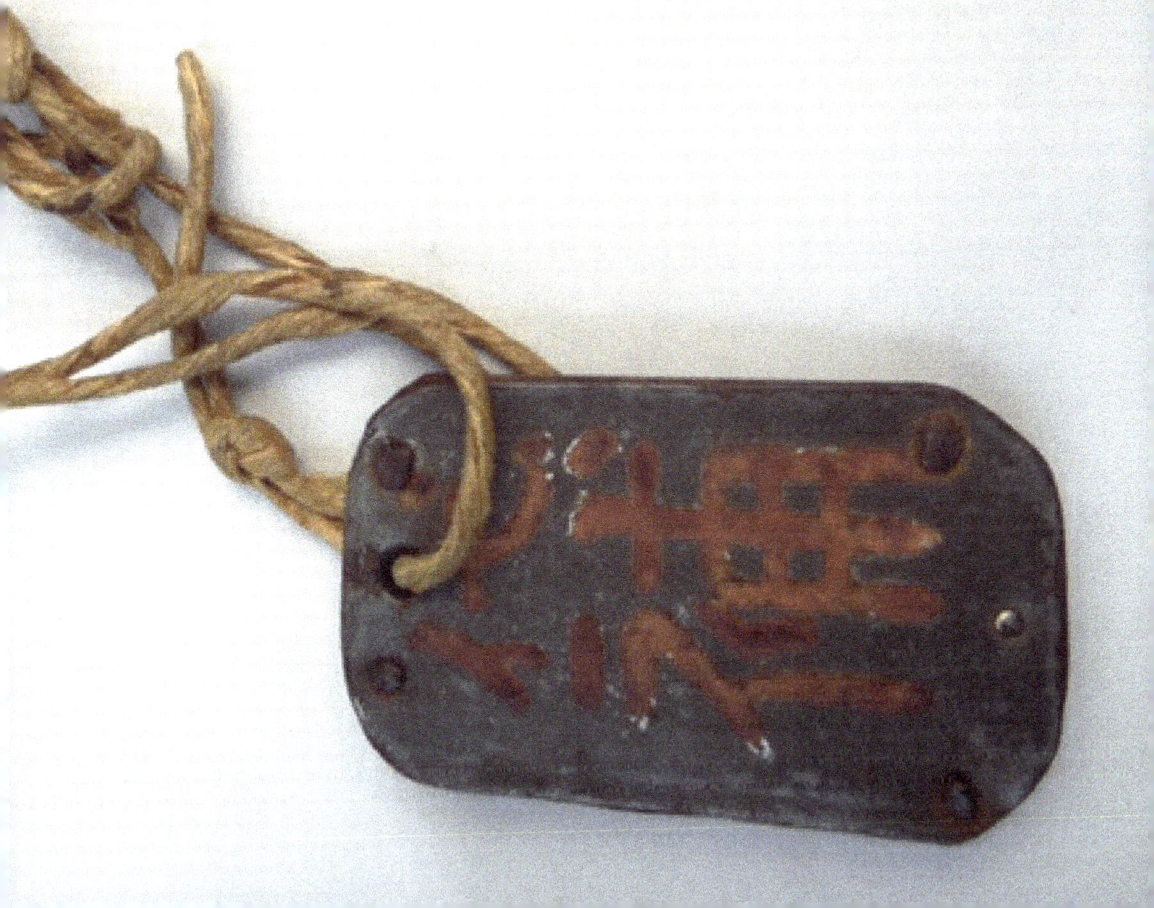

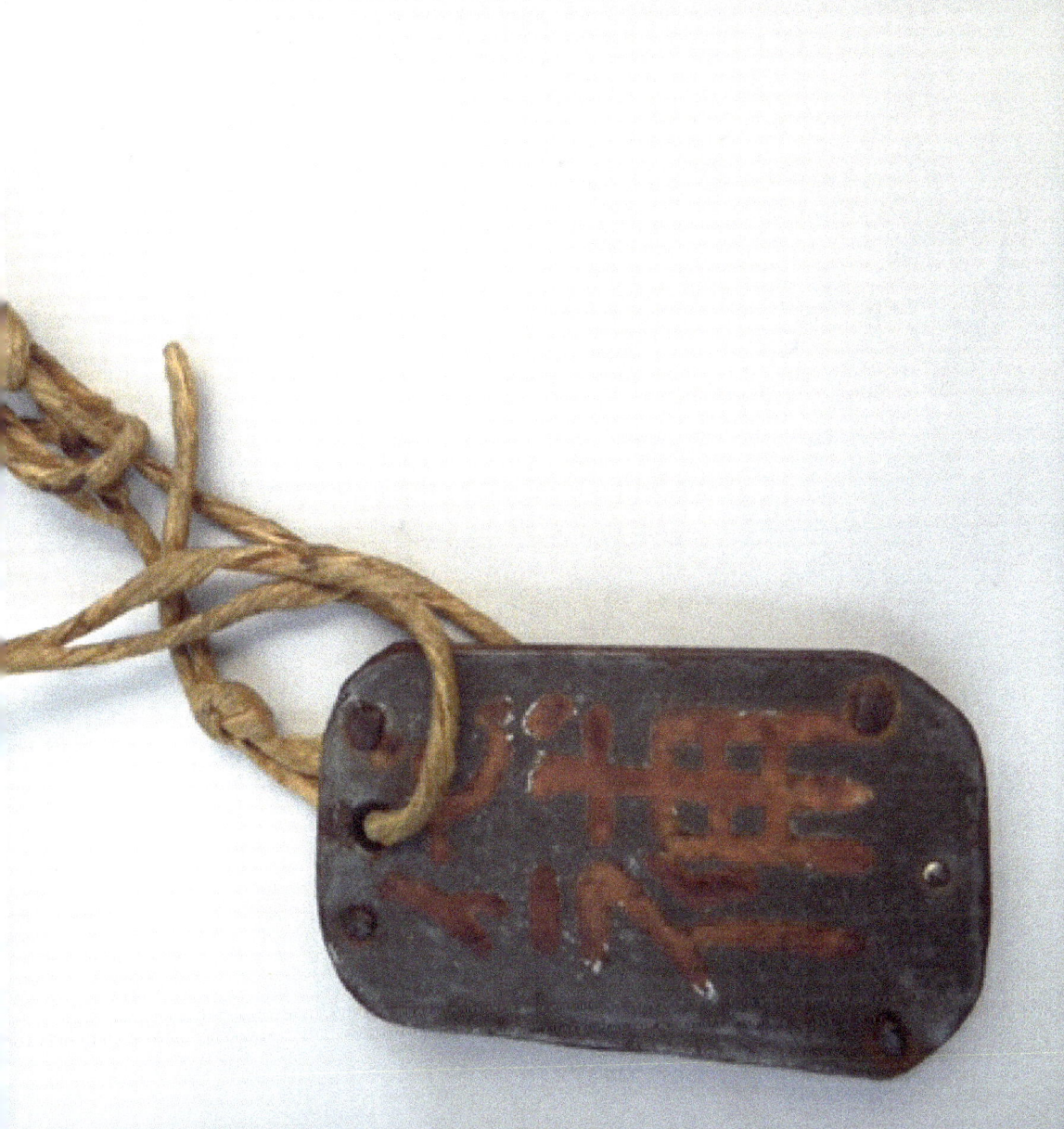

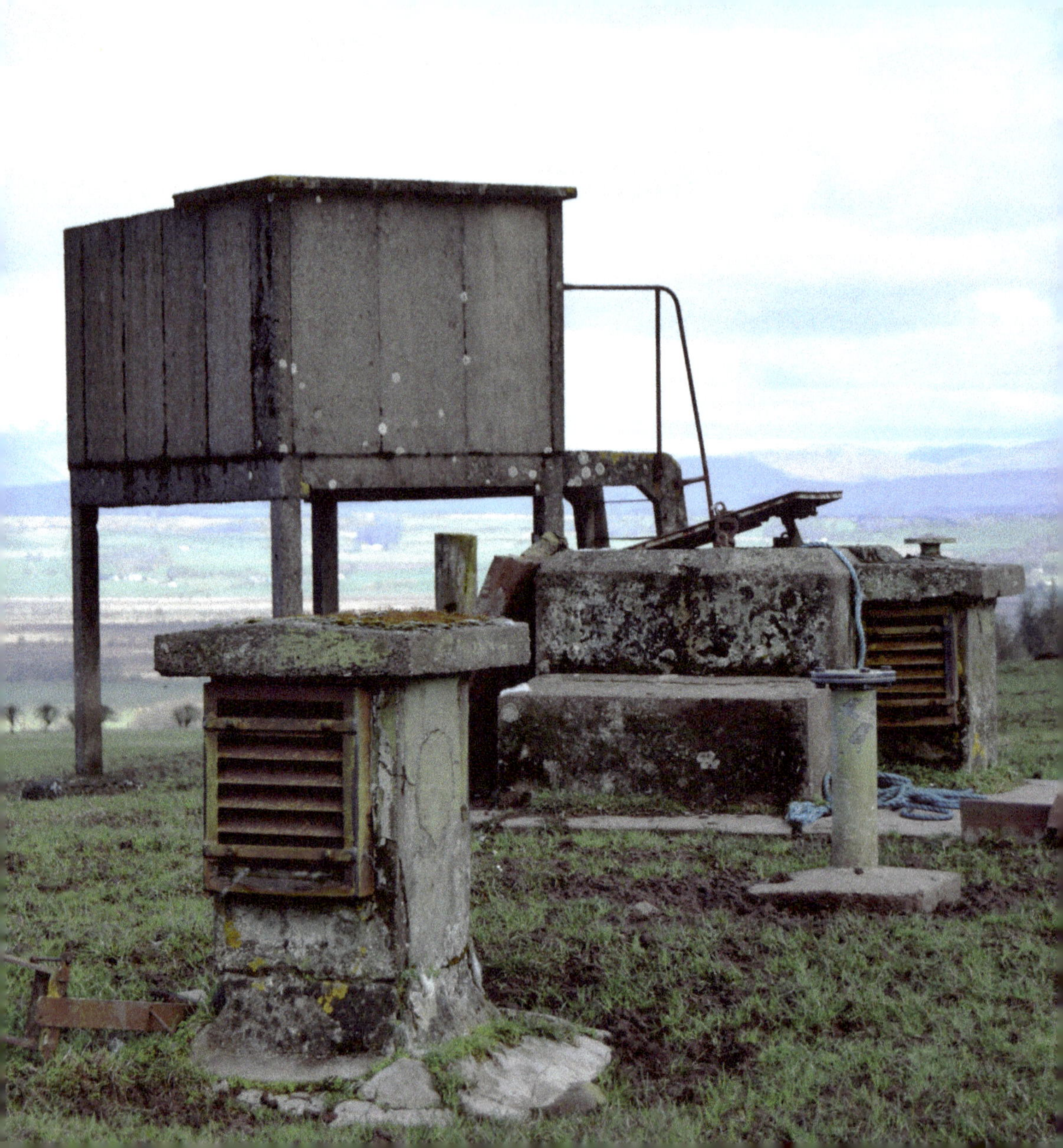

Stirling and the Cold War

During the Second World War, the Royal Observer Corps (ROC) volunteers provided detailed tracking information on German aircraft and their bombs. In the 1950s, the enemy was now our former allies—the Soviets. NATO was formed to combat this risk. A series of ROC posts were constructed, initially of the 'Orlit' type, as shown in the photograph of Kippen ROC Post. This raised tower allowed them to report to the gun positions to the north of Glasgow, including one at Mugdock Country Park (54.3 NS 5436177259). Kippen soon became part of a series of underground Observation Posts which were created across the country, when the Russians developed Atomic bombs. The closest ROC post is just to the east of Stirling on the hill behind the bus depot (54.4 NS 81961 89957). On the surface of both Kippen and Bannockburn, you will find a hatch covering the entrance ladder, ventilation shafts, and a pole for attaching instruments. Underground, there was room for several ROC volunteers, with desks, maps, bunk-beds and chemical toilets. They had supplies for a fortnight.

Various Western spies helped the Soviets upgrade their atomic weapons to thermonuclear missiles with such high yields that survival would be unlikely, so spotting the direction of flash etc. became largely irrelevant. Nevertheless, the ROC continued to exist until 1991, providing uniformed volunteer support to the Regular Forces as well as manning bunkers, with upgraded instrumentation, just in case. Stirling Councillors were given confidential briefings during the Cold War and planned to use various buildings as emergency hospitals, mortuaries, etc. Let us be thankful that the threat of 'Mutually Assured Destruction' kept the peace between the West and the Soviets.

Follow the main road through Kippen and take the right fork down the unclassified road towards Claylands Farm. The Post is uphill (54.1 NS 63513 94236) and can be reached by crossing the small burn at the bridge (54.2 NS 63566 94142). Cars can be parked at the side of the narrow road or at the wide area near the foot of the farm track. The Orlit Post can be seen from the road.

Conclusion

Can one enjoy a book about warfare? We hope that the tone is right: one of respect and exploration. The true witnesses to most of these conflicts are now dead, but perhaps we can best remember their bravery and sacrifice—or confront their folly and greed—using the details and the locations of where these events happened. We hope that this small book has made a contribution to understanding the long and often bloody series of conflicts to control or utilise the Forth.

Warfare and conflict are still with us and, as we write, there are conflicts around the world from Afghanistan to Yemen. As a species we continue to invade, rape and kill, and of course heroes continue to rise to defend their homelands and allies. We pray for peace and for the innocent men, women and children whose lives have been turned upside down and often ended by warfare all so often instigated by greedy or incompetent politicians, who consume people's lives as pieces in a board game.

In the words of the Argyll's motto, *Ne Obliviscaris*: 'Do Not Forget'.

Endnotes

1. All of these Roman structures were erected by soldiers of the Legions, like Legio II Augusta, while the garrisons were made up of Auxiliary units, such as the Spaniards who held Ardoch.

2. The description and depiction of native peoples from the Caledonians to the Picts as naked and later on tattooed is a common theme in both Roman and Pictish carvings and while this does make them barbarous, we think they or perhaps a specific warrior caste probably did fight in the buff.

3. Roman forts tended to follow a standard plan. They were playing-card shaped rectangles with rounded corners. There was a rampart with defensive ditches outside and a walled palisade with four gates into the buildings themselves. These were grouped around two roadways, one down the centre of the long axis and the other, Via Principalis, set about one third of the way across. The troops were housed in barrack blocks for each Century (of eighty soldiers) in rooms of eight men, the Contubernium or 'tenting together'.

    Marching camps followed the same pattern with the palisade being replaced by a system of pointed wooden stakes (sudis) which were combined to form the equivalent of a barbed-wire entanglement. Leather tents were carried by mules, with one to each Contubernium, and were laid out in the same way each day. To illustrate, the First Century was always bottom left and the tents were set up in numbered sequence. In this way, everyone knew their way around even in the dark.

    Jim thinks that there was a morale and even spiritual aspect to this. The men were carrying Rome with them as they travelled into unknown territory, lifting-up their home-town and taking it with them to the next location, where the men of each Century would dig the same section of their ditch each time the camp was being re-established. They would then erect their leather house in the same place, before 'tenting together'. The famous punishment of decimation, where a tenth of the unit was killed by the others was probably based on the Contubernium, with lots drawn and the loser being beaten to death by his tent-mates.

4. The remaining Britons held the area south of the Forth and Clyde for centuries, with Dumbarton (the Fortress of the Britons) as their western capital. They were subject to invasion by the English-speaking Northumbrians from the south and the Gaelic speaking Scots from Argyll (Dal Riata).

5. In 2023, a large, carved stone ball was recovered by local man Douglas Todd. At the time of writing, it is being assessed by the Stirling Smith Museum and Art Gallery, but is probably one of Edward I's trebuchet balls!

6. Jim believes that he has an explanation for the recorded 'kneeling' of the Scots army before the battle, which must have appeared unusual since both armies were Catholic. The Monymusk reliquary, containing the bones of St Columba, was the 'Brecbennach', the holy battle ensign of Scotland. As it was processed before the troops, they would genuflect in turn—a kind of reverential Mexican Wave.

7. Another first for Stirling is the earliest record of the use of a gun in Scotland from our court records on the 9th May 1549!

8. Jim believes that there is a need to re-examine the location of the battle since the Jacobite objective was to cross the Forth and the Redcoats' task was to deny them the use of the main road south (roughly along today's railway line). Also, while we do not know the size/frontages of the Jacobite force, British Army records and drill-books still survive and it is clear that the cavalry wings took up more space than the infantry, and we can visualise the spacing of the British Army. Disappointingly, the best map of the battle was in two

parts and the only part still in possession of the National Library shows the Jacobite move from Kinbuck towards Dunblane; the half with the battle itself is missing.

At the time, the Sheriffmuir battle was named 'The Battle of Dunblain', rather than Sheriffmuir, since the main strategic issue for the Redcoats was stopping the Jacobite rebels reaching the ford at Kildean by blocking their passage on the main road through Dunblane. Given the numbers of Government forces and the space required for each Regiment, it seems clear that the British Army deployed with its left-wing cavalry next to the River Allan (probably on the Holme Hill) with the infantry in line along the road which passes the Hydro and the right wing cavalry, including the Scots Greys, stretching beyond.

They would earlier have deployed a cavalry piquet on the high-ground to the east of today's 'Gathering Stone' to observe to the north. This piquet was described at the time as 'a body of the enemies horse' which has led some to place the redcoats out on the muir from the beginning, but this seems very unlikely given the Army's need to cover the road south through Dunblane. When they realised that the road was blocked by the government forces, the Jacobites swung to the east, onto the higher ground to continue their move to the Kildean ford. The Redcoats rushed up the hill to meet them and the battle began. Jim believes that the centre of the battle was much closer to 'Dunblain' than the existing monuments suggest. What is certain is that a much outnumbered Government army (3,000 vs 6,000) defeated the Jacobites.

> 'The success on either side is doubtful to this day,
> And all that can be said is, both armies ran away;
> And on whichsoever side success lay it was toward the Government,
> And to allay all doubts about which party won, we must feel content.
>
> *The Battle of Sheriffmuir* by William Topaz McGonagall

Image Credits

All images are from the authors' collections unless otherwise stated.

Frontispiece: Stirling's Burgh Seal on the Central Library (NS 79529 93386), which mentions Scots and Britons (or brute Scots!), reflecting a time when Stirling was not fully Scottish!

Page 1: The wynding links of the Forth from Dumyat.

Page 2: A 6,000 year old flint arrowhead, currently in the Stirling Smith Museum and Art Gallery.

Page 3: Excavating Neolithic polissoirs.

Page 6: The Excavation of Fairy Knowe in 1868, courtesy of the Society of Antiquaries of Scotland and reproduced by kind permission of the copyright holder.

Page 7: A Bronze Age Spear Tip. Courtesy of Dr Gemma Cruickshanks of the National Museum of Scotland and reproduced by kind permission of the copyright holder.

Page 10: The Ruined Walls of Leckie Broch on top of its amazing rock art.

Page 11: A Celtic Horse Terret Ring. Courtesy of Alan George Baxter and reproduced by kind permission of the copyright holder.

Page 14: The amazing Ardoch Roman Fort from the air. Courtesy of Dr Andrew Tibbs and reproduced by kind permission of the copyright holder.

Page 15: The Antonine Wall from the Roman fort at Rough Castle. Image is Copyright © Lairich Rig at Geograph UK <*geograph.org.uk/p/925797*> and is licensed under the Creative Commons Attribution Share-Alike 2.0 Generic license <*https://creativecommons.org/licenses/by-sa/2.0/deed.en*>.

Page 18: The Lilia at Rough Castle. Image is Copyright © Lairich Rig at Geograph UK <*geograph.org.uk/p/925844*> and is licensed under the Creative Commons Attribution Share-Alike 2.0 Generic license <*https://creativecommons.org/licenses/by-sa/2.0/deed.en*>.

Page 19: Dr Louisa Campbell's gruesome reconstruction of the Bridgeness Slab. Courtesy of Dr Campbell, and reproduced by kind permission of the copyright holder.

Page 22: Fit for An Emperor: The Craigarnhall Marching Camp, by Therese McCormick and reproduced by kind permission of the copyright holder.

Page 23: A Maeatian Warrior. The Tulloch Man Carving, found near Perth, after Aberdeen University by Therese McCormick and reproduced by kind permission of the copyright holder.

Page 26: Drip Bridge: The site of a Massacre of Picts?

Page 27: Dumyat: The fort of the Maeatae.

Page 30: The Abbey Craig from the Forth.

Page 31: The Rendering of the Burgh Seal at the Stirling Smith Art Gallery and Museum (NS 79081 93499).

Page 34: The grave of an unknown friar from Stirling Dominican Priory.

Page 35: Sir William Wallace at Stirling Athenaeum (NS 79579 93433).

Page 38: Ladies Rock; a promontory in Stirling's Valley Cemetery.

Page 39: Wolf at the door: the largest ever trebuchet. Illustration Copyright © Bob Marshall, and reproduced by kind permission of the copyright holder.

Page 42: Milton Ford, across which brave de Bohun made his last, fatal charge.

Page 43: The Abbey Ford: the most important in Scotland.

Page 46: The path to victory: Balquiderrock Wood.

Page 47: Allan Primary School Bastion: The best-preserved bastion on Scotland's best-preserved city wall!

Page 50: Doune's crossed pistols. The old town sign, currently in Doune Post Office (NN 72716 01585) and reproduced by their kind permission.

Page 51: The Kilsyth Victor: The first Marquis of Montrose. Courtesy of The Argyll and Sutherland Highlanders Museum in Stirling Castle (NS 78965 94069), and reproduced by kind permission of the copyright holder.

Page 54: Pock marks on tower indicating musket ball damage to The Church of Holy Rude, perhaps caused by the last siege of Stirling Castle by Bonnie Prince Charlie or more likely Cromwell's siege of 1651.

Page 55: Stirling Bridge: Scotland's best-preserved medieval bridge.

Page 58: Hero or Villain? Stirling's Rob Roy statue (NS 79441 93384).

Page 59: Colonel John Blackadder: staunch anti-Jacobite and slave owner? Image from the National Galleries of Scotland.

Page 62: Bonnie Prince Charlie's Jacobites blow up St Ninians Kirk! Courtesy of the collection of The Stirling Smith Art Gallery & Museum, and reproduced by kind permission of the copyright holder.

Page 63: The Earl of Dunmore's family crest at Dunmore, showing a liberated slave.

Page 66: Lieutenant General Samuel Graham, from his biography, *Memoir of General Graham*, with notices of the campaigns in which he was engaged from 1779 to 1801.

Page 67: Portrait of Tipu Sultan by an anonymous Indian artist in Mysore, ca.1790-1800. Wikimedia Commons.

Page 70: Airthrey Castle: built using Indian resources.

Page 71: A Waterloo Man: Colour Sergeant William McGibbon's grave.

Page 74: A Member of The Thin Red Line Private Mathew Murphy's Grave.

Page 75: The Henderson Brothers' Family Home, Allan Park House, Stirling.

Page 78: General Sir John Alexander Ewart: Hero of Lucknow. Image from the National Galleries of Scotland.

Page 79: The Argyll and Sutherland Highlanders Memorial: Statues on Stirling Castle's forecourt. Image is Copyright © Andrew Smith at Geograph UK <*geograph.org.uk/p/192299*> and is licensed under the Creative Commons Attribution Share-Alike 2.0 Generic license <*https://creativecommons.org/licenses/by-sa/2.0/deed.en*>.

Page 82: A Brand New Sopwith 1½ Strutter: Sophie the Strutter, as flown by 44 Squadron, built by Mike Harper and his colleagues in the Aviation Preservation Society of Scotland. Image courtesy of Mike Harper, and reproduced by kind permission of the copyright holder.

Page 83: Former Drill Hall, Princess Street. Image is Copyright © Alex McGregor at Geograph UK <*geograph.org.uk/p/4053199*> and is licensed under the Creative Commons Attribution Share-Alike 2.0 Generic license <https://creativecommons.org/licenses/by-sa/2.0/deed.en>.

Page 86: Secret Destruction: The munitions stores at Bandeath.

Page 87: Fallen Heroes: The Stirling War Memorial.

Page 90: The St Paul's altar frontal, which Private McChord helped to make. Image Copyright © The Chapter of St Paul's Cathedral, and appears by kind permission of the copyright holder.

Page 91: The remains of a World War II Polish hero's jacket? Courtesy of Dr Gabriela Ingle, and reproduced by kind permission of the copyright holder.

Page 94: A Home Guard training bunker on Abbey Craig being dug by Sue MacKay.

Page 95: Visions of Home: POW Otto Laub's painting of Cologne Cathedral. This survived the war, but Otto would not know that till he got home. Courtesy of the collection of the Stirling Smith Art Gallery & Museum, and reproduced by kind permission of the copyright holder.

Page 98: Who Dares Wins: The Sir David Stirling War Memorial.

Page 99: HMS *Mounsey* as it appears on Malcolm 'Bunty' McPhee McColl's Memorial.

Page 102: The End of the Nazis Started Here: The Atlantic Wall Replica.

Page 103: The nephews of Henri De La Bastita at the unveiling of his memorial.

Page 106: WW2 Far East prisoner of war identity tag which belonged to RSM Alexander 'Sandy' Munnoch, 2nd Battalion Argyll and Sutherland Highlanders. Image is courtesy of The Argyll and Sutherland Highlanders Museum and is reproduced by kind permission of the copyright holder.

Page 107: Watching for Armageddon: The Kippen ROC Post.

About the Authors

Dr Murray Cook is Stirling Council's Archaeologist. He lives in the city with a long-suffering wife, three teenage girls and two pesky but loveable cats. He has undertaken numerous excavations across the region and published over 50 books and articles. He won a Stirling's Provost Award in 2018 for his work for the Council, where he has helped raise over £300,000 to be spent on community archaeology and research, and was even invited to see the Queen at Holyrood Palace, along with a few hundred others! He has appeared on several TV programmes, and has sometime even been paid. He writes a regular column in the *Stirling Observer* upon which this this book is based, is an Honorary Research Fellow at Stirling University, a Fellow of the Society of Antiquaries of Scotland, runs an occasional course at Forth Valley College on Stirling and likes to do it in ditches (archaeology that is!). He also co-runs regular training digs open to all under the name *Rampart Scotland*. If you share Murray's passion for the past why not look up his weekly blog, *Stirling's Archaeology*? It's free to join.

Jim Roche returned to Scotland in 1995 with his wife Morven and their three children, and has lived in Stirling since then. They now have two grandchildren. After graduating in Physics at Glasgow University in 1974, Jim worked in Operations Management before studying Marketing at Lancaster University.

Jim worked in the marketing of new products for Cadbury, where he launched the Wispa bar (the original was far better than today's version). He became a Board Director of Bacardi-Martini, and remembers crossing the Atlantic on Concorde to attend an urgent meeting in New York. In business, Jim has worked with a wide range of organisations which have included food, software development, telecoms, games and virtual reality, forestry estates, electronics and precision engineering.

Since retiring, he has served as a Director for various charities. When he's not 'walking the ground' with an old map in hand to better understand battlefields, he is reading personal diaries and soldier's memories. Jim was a founding member of Wargame Developments in 1981. This is a group devoted to simulating historical military and political events using everything from drama and debate to maps and even toy soldiers. It is from these discussions that he became convinced about the need to understand the religious and social motivations of people in the past and the importance of unit frontages and supply in understanding historical battles.

He has several published articles on military themes as well as on Church history. Jim has volunteered at various archaeological digs, most particularly at the Roman frontier at the Gask Ridge over several seasons. His 'surprising fact' is that he was once an extra in a Bollywood movie.

For details of new and forthcoming books from Extremis Publishing, including our monthly podcasts, please visit our official website at:

www.extremispublishing.com

EXTREMIS publishing
Welcome to Extremis Publishing
Our Books
Awarded Independent Publishing Company of the Year at the Scotland Prestige Awards 2021/22, 2022/23 and 2023/24

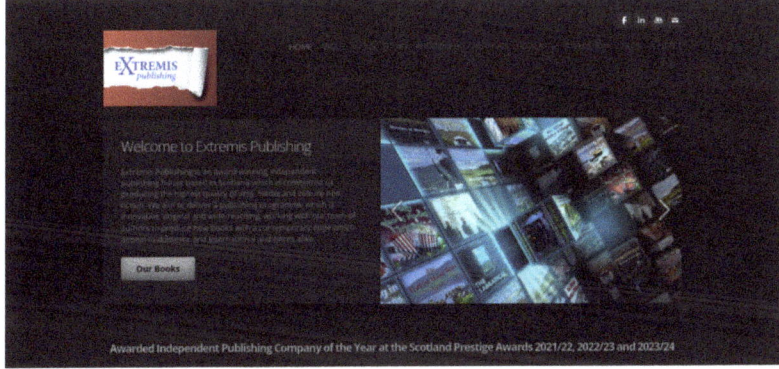

or follow us on social media at:

www.facebook.com/extremispublishing

www.linkedin.com/company/extremis-publishing-ltd-/

www.ingramcontent.com/pod-product-compliance
Lightning Source LLC
Chambersburg PA
CBHW042352070526
44585CB00028B/2905